To my Son and Mother, for all their love.

HARRIS ROSEN

CONTENTS

ACKNOWLEDGMENTS

Thank you those who inspired me behind the scenes to produce this book. I appreciate your support, friendship, guidance and understanding.

HARRIS ROSEN

PREFACE

Every tale has a backstory, and my interviews with 213 are no different. We're talking, two five hour flights to LAX to a cancelled upon arrival interview deep in Mexican and El Salvadorian gang territory. A stare down with Nate Dogg on the top of a mountain with no cell reception while spending a day on the set of the Groupie Luv" video shoot, and a second cancelled Snoop Dogg interview.

Anything Snoop Dogg has been relevant and in demand ever since he connected with Dr Dre and recorded "Deep Cover". Snoop Dogg left Death Row Records in 1998 and signed a three album contract with Master P's No Limit Records. He shaved Doggy off his name, spent the next three years in the studio, and sold over five million solo albums. Upon fulfilling his contractual obligation to No Limit, Snoop Dogg transitioned from gangster to pimp, elevating his ascent into the pop culture icon he is today.

Warren G inaugurated the G-funk Era with "Regulate" featuring Nate Dogg on the **Above The Rim the Soundtrack** and **Regulate... G Funk Era**. The album debuted at #2 on the Billboard Top 200 Album Chart selling 176,000 its opening week. Warren G and Nate Dogg forever synonymous with the definition of G-funk and its folklore.

The close friendship of Snoop Dogg, Nate Dogg, and Warren G dates back to their teen years in Long Beach. Snoop Dogg and Warren G grew up together selling candy and playing Football, and Snoop Dogg and Nate Dogg went to High School together. Warren G was a DJ following in the footsteps of his older half-brother, Dr Dre, Snoop rapped, and Nate sang hooks. They began to jam together using records, turntables, and a microphone.

Snoop graduated from High School in 1989 and had no interest in the 9-5 grind. One of their local homeboys, Money B, made beats, so Warren G hooked him up with Snoop and Nate Dogg. Together, they drove to his house and recorded "Long Beach Is A Mutherfucker." One week later, 200-300 people in the neighbourhood heard it, and they started selling cassette tapes for $5. They recorded another song with Money B and then worked with a DJ on the east-side of the LBC out of the VIP Records studio. Slice stepped up the song production and added a "bigger beat." Soon LC, a producer from the west-side of the LBC joined in. Snoop recorded "Gangster's Life" with Nate Dogg, mixed with LL Cool J's "The Boomin' System." Warren G played the tape for Dr Dre, and the rest is history.

Behind the scenes, fans yearned for 213 to make music

together, again. They had recorded a handful of songs together since their initial forays in the studio, but other artists featured on the tracks. It took until 1999, for the trio to reunite in the studio and record "Game Don't Wait" for the Warren G solo album, *I Want It All*, however, it was the remix produced by Dr Dre with special guest Xzibit that blew up. In 2001, they recorded "Yo' Sassy Ways" for Warren G's fourth solo album *The Return of the Regulator*.

213 returned in 2003 with "So Fly" to set off *Bigg Snoop Dogg Presents Welcome To Tha Chuuch Vol. 2* mixtape. It became the unofficial lead single for *The Hard Way*, and the group performed the song live on BET's 106 & Park. When word of a 213 album leaked, fans were excited, and the anticipation level was high. I phoned TVT Canada and spoke with Rebecca Black, who put the wheels in motion and landed us an exclusive cover feature interview and photo shoot in Los Angeles, and flights booked. Then the call came.

213 had to appear in fresh gear for the cover shoot, and we had to pay their stylist, April Roomet. The next day, Photographer Craig Boyko and I were checked in at YYZ, when Kurupt stared us in the eyes. The cover feature of The Source June 2004 issue, *Inside The Breakup of Hip-Hop Crews: KURUPT The End of DPG. Death Row's Last Inmate States His Case.*

The 213 interview and photo shoot scheduled for 4:00 p.m., inside a Central Los Angeles, Echo Park, studio. Unfortunately, we misjudged L.A. traffic and arrived at 5:00 p.m. and 213 were in a rush to leave. Before its current gentrification, Echo Park is known for its massive presence of Mexican and El Salvadorian gangs. Snoop Dogg, Warren G, Nate Dogg and their respective crews, did not want to be there after dark. There would be time for photos, but, no interview. 213 stylist, April Roomet set each of them up with fresh kicks and a limited edition NFL Heritage sweater. (Years later, I hand Snoop Dogg a copy of the issue. He stood transfixed, staring at the jersey.)

Craig Boyko flew home to YYZ the next day. I headed south to Huntington Beach and waited. Ten days later, June 30, 2004, Rob Harris and I drove up the coast to Santa Monica. We were invited to do the 213 interviews on the set of the "Groupie Luv" video shoot. Let me get this straight. A Snoop Dogg, Warren G and New Dogg video shoot, directed by Chris Robinson, for a song called "Groupie Luv".

There is no cell phone service.

A big budget video shoot, throughout a secluded sprawling luxurious private home on the top of a coastal mountain range parallel to the Pacific Ocean. The set was in full motion upon our arrival. Dozens of beautiful bikini-clad models standing by in the wings waiting for their time to shine. Director Chris Robinson was orchestrating the day perched in his Director's chair, flanked by a cadre of assistants. Rob and I hung in the shadows taking it all in, until being summoned to interview Warren G and Nate Dogg.

My approach to interviews is to ask the artist what I don't know. Warren G is a superstar producer, and I wanted to know why he did not produce any songs for the album. I asked Nate Dogg about his place in music, the business, President George W. Bush and the war in Iraq. When I asked a few questions about Kurupt's allegations in The Source, like did Snoop Dogg not treat his people right? And that's when Nate Dogg got salty on me. The interview was ending on a positive note as he spoke of his passion for the NBA.

Snoop Dogg was coming up next. Two hours later, we are approached by the lead publicist. Snoop is busy working on a promo with MLB. Rob and I head down the hill to eat on the beach. One hour later, we arrive back on set told Snoop is unavailable. No Snoop Dogg interview. I fly home to YYZ two days later.

"So Fly" was released as an official single on July 6, 2004, and hit number 2 on the Billboard Bubbling Under Hot 100 singles chart. Three weeks later, following much behind the scenes negotiations, Snoop Dogg is on the phone for an interview with Jason Richards. 213 appear on the cover of the September 2004, fall edition. **The Hard Way** finally released on August 17, 2004. It entered the Billboard Top 200 at number 4 and took the top spot on the R&B/Hip-Hop album chart.

There you have it. The Behind The Music Tales of 213.

Enjoy!

FOREWORD

(Long Beach, CA) Check your phone. If the area code doesn't tip you off then maybe the global positioning system will. Even on the GPS of pop culture, where real places usually get transformed into iconic themes, this is the 'hood. Not just any 'hood, but the 'hood. A stretch of the glitzy and grimy where, during the 1980s, an uneasy collaboration between the film studios and record labels of La La Land met a handful of residents from the streets of Long Beach, Watts, Inglewood, and Compton. To birth an urban-Americana fascination with gang culture that makes James G. Robinson look like diet legend. And while the Hughes Brothers and John Singleton take some credit for mythologising the west coast to the eye, the fix on all things gangster first came through the evolution of the ear. That sound was G-funk.

Back when it first swept east, Snoop Dogg, Nate Dogg, and Warren G were among its most formidable pioneers: the rapper, the hook man, the producer. Now, more than a decade later, they've rejoined forces as 213 for one of the most anticipated albums of the year. Don't anticipate retro G. Instead, with Warren G taking a lead role on the mic and the production duties farmed out. To Kanye West, Hi-Tek, DJ Pooh, Missy Elliott, Fredwreck, J-Hen, Michael Angelo, B Sharp,

Quazedelic, Niggarochi, that Chill, Lil 1/2 Dead, and Nottz. Think of **The Hard Way** as the 2.0 of pimp-crawl.

G-funk has changed. Its place in your heart remains.

Chuuuch!

CHAPTER 1

THE HARD WAY

The 213 album is long overdue. Why now?

Snoop Dogg: Why now? Probably because we been waiting for so long actually to put out a 213 record, and now that we are able to do it, it's appropriate for right now. So, that's what the feeling is all about. Us expressing what we feel, that's what we feel.

What is the focus of this 213 record?

Snoop Dogg: Just tryin' to make records that just made us feel good, that represent what we was going through at the time. We got a couple of records on there that are a little bit deeper than others, but for the most part just partying. We had a lot of people in the studio, a lot of smoke, a lot of drink. You know, the atmosphere was a party.

What is your role on the 213 project?

Warren G: My role with this project is I'm the Producer/MC.

Many fans posting on 213music.net were upset that you did not have more of a handle on this album's production?

Warren G: I can't call that. I got a track on there. It's called "Sassy Ways." We're gonna put that on the album. It's off the chain. My guys, they wanted to go with different producers and get new music. I'm gonna roll with 'em whichever way we gonna do it. So that's how we did it.

What's the 213 album about to you, and your reason for being on it?

Warren G: My reason for being on it is because I'm with my friends. I'm with Snoop, I'm with Nate, and we weren't able to do that before. So it's just like I'm doing it for my friends and me.

But you're Warren G. You're the DJ, the man behind the G-funk sound. There's a little G-funk on the album, but, when you got the guy who invented it, the King of it, isn't it odd?

Warren G: What? (Laughs)

You're not doing more production.

Warren G: (Laughs) Hey, I mean, that's why we decided to do it. I would have loved to put more tracks on there but, like I'm saying and I said, the guys wanted to get a different flavour from different other producers. I ain't gonna argue about the whole thing. I will just roll with the punches.

Does commerce come before art in this case?

Warren G: You ought to ask him this question. (Laughs) I'm straight, man. I ain't tripping.

Why was Warren G not more involved with the production?

Snoop Dogg: I believe he probably wanted to showcase more of his rap skills on this record. You know, come on up out of that shell as far as just being known as a producer. So he felt if he didn't produce on the record that would take that talk away, as far as he's just a producer, as he didn't produce on the record and he sounds good as a rapper.

What is your take on the 213 album lyrics? You're talking about the summertime, groupie love.

Nate Dogg: Just having fun. We took our whole, everything we was doing, whenever we came in that was on our mind that day, we just did it. We was having fun, and that was it. A whole lot of fun on some days. A little too much fun.

Why is the album on TVT?

Nate Dogg: 'Cause they gave us the money. (Laughs) They wrote a cheque.

CHAPTER 2

WHAT HAVE YOU DONE FOR ME LATELY?

Ten years after Warren G introduced "Regulate" and officially branded the G-funk Era, the members of 213 were still omnipresent in the studio working on new music and assisting others to produce, rap and sing on singles and album tracks. Sadly, most of the music appeared on under the radar compilation albums and mixtapes. With the long-awaited 213 album finally set to see the light of day, interest in their music and lifestyle began to make a bit of a comeback, and Snoop Dogg's spiritual advisor, Bishop Don Magic Juan, was along for the ride.

***

What has Warren G been up to lately?

Warren G: Working on the 213 with Snoop and Nate, working on my solo at the same time, and just being me. Producing tracks 'cause I'm focusing on production more than being an MC, so that's kind of what I'm doing.

Back in the day, you were killing it: Regulators with Nate Dogg; you had Wayniac and Tripp Locc, The Twinz; The Dove Shack. What happened to the whole Warren G empire?

Warren G: I'm working with the 5 Footaz right now as we speak. The Dove Shack wasn't my group. They signed under Def Jam, and Chris Lighty asked me if I could let them represent G-funk, and I was just, like, cool. So I let them do that. But they were not my group. The Twinz was my group. The Twinz is working on independent records right now. They was working with Snoop and them. Now they started working with Daz. They are doing independent records. Like I said, the 5 Footaz, I've been doing stuff on them lately, been doing stuff for myself. I got this youngster, this new youngster named DS. He's out of Long Beach. He's incredible. And I got an R&B artist named Junie that's off the chain.

What keeps you going? Where do you want to take the music? Do you want to flip it up, or will you always be Nate on the chorus?

Nate Dogg: At this point, I'm real happy with doing choruses. I'm real happy with doing what I do, but I want my next album to be successful 'cause I feel like I want people to recognise what I do as a solo artist, which is why I got a good time to plug it right now. Dr Dre is doing the whole album, so it's going to be very different. But right now we don't want to get sidetracked from the 213 album that's coming out. But yeah, I'm doing different stuff, just trying to grow with my music. I'm happy though where I'm at, very happy.

What's a typical day for Nate Dogg?

Nate Dogg: Now I'm resting, man. I got about two weeks left of resting and then it's work, work, work. Every day I'm just trying to get something done. I'm trying to get on everybody's album. I want to be on Stevie Wonder's album, Michael Jackson's album. Them kind of albums.

Are you locked down to Atlantic or other deals?

Nate Dogg: As a solo artist, yeah, I have another record deal. This is a group deal. Gives me an idea. I should start like eight more groups and get eight other cheques. 213, 415 ... (Laughs).

Talk about the Star Trak deal with Pharrell.

Snoop Dogg: Actually, it's not a deal. It's just him and me coming together on a collaboration, a joint venture where he'll do half the record, and I'm doing half the record.

He's singing, and you're handling he raps?

Snoop Dogg: Like, a little bit of both, you know what

I'm saying? Some songs I'm singing, some songs he rappin'. Just the best of both worlds.

Can we expect to see Snoop Dogg in more movies?

Snoop Dogg: Oh yeah. That's what you can expect in a real way. I'm looking at a couple of scripts right now. I'm just gonna take my time and pick the best one.

What about your upcoming album?

Bishop Don Magic Juan: One thing about it is it's coming out on Avatar Records. My CD is gonna be some old school music. I mean, real live. Snoop Dogg gave me a couple of uptempo tunes, so it's gonna be going on. Y'all get that on Avatar Records. The ***Archbishop Don Magic Juan, Green is for the Money & Gold is for the Honey's Vol. 1.*** Chuuch! Now that's pimping, and the only player ever been signed to William Morris Agency. Now y'all check that out. Preach!

CHAPTER 3

G-FUNK TO THE FUTURE

Shouldn't Warren G be more prevalent?

Nate Dogg: What I think you don't understand, man, is G-funk is evolving. All these questions you asking, they real cool and all, but you forget – you looking for a G-Funk sound that was in ten years ago. We are evolving now into something else. I think you should wait to hear the album and hear what's going on. This is not somewhere where you stay stuck in one place. You have to evolve around and do different things. You can't have one sound and continue and expect to grow and expect people to go with you if you in the same place. You have to move. So that's what we are doing. We're trying to bring something different to the table and show Warren G off not only as a DJ but as a rap artist, so that's what we are doing as far as 213. And Warren G and Nate Dogg created this G-Funk shit, and you hear it on... just go listen to the radio. It's everywhere. Every time you hear me, you hear Warren G. That's who we are, that's where the sound came from. Everybody in the world is at my doorstep right now wanting a song. Everybody! Ask them when you interview 'em.

What about the Regulators? A lot of people have been

waiting on an album by Warren G and Nate Dogg.

Nate Dogg: A Regulators album?

People are posting it on your site.

Nate Dogg: Hold on for a minute. Warren G!

Warren G: I have no idea.

Nate Dogg: Shit, give it back to me. That's what I was gonna say. (Laughter) You don't know, do you?

Warren G: Hell no. Me and Nate, we got a lot of songs together. Shit, one of these days it might happen. You never know.

Nate Dogg: I want to get one of these songs too, for my album.

What's the Warren G production flavour like these days? Where are you taking it?

Warren G: I'm gonna take it to the top. It's more soulful with hard, kicking drums. That gangster groove, that melody.

Who is doing it now? Who are you feeling?

Warren G: I like Slum Village, whoever does their tracks, he's incredible. I think they do it. Yeah, they incredible. I like The Roots, Scott Storch, Kanye West,

Warren G, and Dr Dre.

What do you think happened to the Long Beach scene and where it's at now with the artists?

Nate Dogg: As far as Long Beach, we need to step our game up. The World has a lot of people that's making music, and Long Beach has a lot of talented artists out there. We need to step our game up. We got into the mode where so many people from Long Beach made it, to where everybody is like all you got to do is be from Long Beach to make it, but it takes a lot of talent to make it no matter where you from. They need to focus on their talent and not focus on who has made it before them that can help them.

Warren G: Times moves fast as hell.

Nate Dogg: Yeah, and once you get in the door, it's like you can get in the door but once you get in the door, now you got to perform. You got to know how to do your job before you want the job. That's what we are doing. We are letting the tail wag the dog. We'll be all right.

Are you happy with this thing you created and where it is right now?

Warren G: I'm very happy. G-funk ain't went nowhere. It's still here.

CHAPTER 4

THE BUSINESS

If you were teaching music school management, what lessons would you deliver?

Nate Dogg: The first lesson everybody needs to get is a lesson in patience. Don't think you are gonna be successful immediately and don't get happy when you get a record deal. That just means you just got a job and a job where you got to earn your cheque. You get paid by what you do. A job and not only a job, you just got a deal. A record deal means nothing. We need to focus on being able to feed our families when you get an opportunity. That's another thing – a record deal if you take advantage of that opportunity, and you do something with it.

Is the business treating artists properly these days?

Nate Dogg: Business has never treated uneducated artists properly. If you educate yourself, you get done. As far as your education takes you that's as far as you'll go. If you don't educate yourself about the business, you'll get got. That's just the rules. That's any business.

Are labels turning down talented, intelligent artists because they know the game?

Nate Dogg: I haven't witnessed that myself because a talented artist, it's hard to turn down talent. If they think they're gonna make money, they'll make a deal with you. So what, if you're smart enough to make yourself a little more money. They think you're talented; they're coming after you. I think, what we do as artists, that's up and coming artists, we focus on the wrong part of the business. We focus on getting a real big cheque first and then not realising that that cheque is recoupable, so we ass out. We into 'em. We get a big ass deal, and we think we got the record company, like 'Yeah, they paying me'. They didn't pay you anything.

How many years did it take you to learn this?

Nate Dogg: Two. The first year I was in the hospital because my asshole was wide open. It was bleeding every day from getting fucked. But after that it was cool. It don't take but only so long to learn. That's what it's all about. A record company did me. I'm sure you know my history, my first record deal I got done up. Yes, sir. But hey, it was also like I said, an opportunity. That first record deal is what got me sitting here talking to you. I was at that place for a certain reason. There it is. I'm here, man. It all worked out.

CHAPTER 5

SALTY

With everything that is happening on an international scale, why do Hip-Hop and R&B artists continue to beef with each other? Why do they carry on with a Jr High mentality calling out names?

Nate Dogg: You said it because they have a mentality that's just they're not bigger. They don't see the big picture. You start off with 'I want to feed my kids, I'm in the gutter, I'm doing bad'. And then when you start doing good you're like,' Oh, I don't like him. I don't like what he is doing'. Then you start trying to chop off his full source. That's something that we have bad. Everybody's competing, but I think it's enough room for all of us to get along and make a whole lot of money. We cut off our money sources by being enemies with people that we should be friends with; I'm not a part of that. I'm Nate. Look at my track record. I've done songs with everybody. Even people that say they don't like each other. They got one thing in common. They all like Nate. I could be a spy. (Laughs)

What's it like working with Snoop?

Nate Dogg: I've been working with Snoop my whole

life. That's who I did my first song with so it's all I know. And he's funny as hell. I guess you know that by now. He's a funny cat. Warren G also. I have a lot of fun. There's no pressure like 'Oh I'm going in here, I got to do this song'. It's like working with friends, so it's a lot easier a whole lot.

It appears a lot of artists are transient who work with Snoop. He works with Warren and then stops working with Warren for a long time, and then Warren is back in the picture when it makes sense. Sort of liking picking up players to use when you want them, NBA style.

Nate Dogg: As far as Snoop? Snoop has a solo career. Situations in your life make you make decisions. You don't be, like, okay, I'm gonna go this one route and if this route don't work I'm gonna keep going with this route, and I'm just gonna run into a brick wall. There's a wall there. You have to figure out a way to go around it, so you have to make decisions in your life that accommodate what's going on in your life, so I don't think anybody was dropped. Everybody had their career going on. Everybody had things going on in their life, and, I think, that's what you do if you're a young entrepreneur. You go out and pursue your money. Anything you have in front of you that you think you can make some money you do it. That's what I'm going to do.

Does Snoop treat you with respect and as a man at all times?

Nate Dogg: My question is if he don't? What does that have to do with me making my money? Snoop Dogg has been my friend and is one of my best friends, to this day. But treat me like a man? I don't understand that. I'm a man. If I was a woman, I guess he'd treat me like a woman. But I'm a man, so he has to treat me like a man.

He'll look you in the eyes, treat you with respect, and give you proper business deals?

Nate Dogg: Yeah, that's my friend. We've been doing this for twelve years, and before that, before it was a business in it. At one time he took some food stamps from me. I ain't gonna tell you about that though. That was bad, like eighty dollars and he brought me back twenty.

Kurupt stated in The Source; Snoop never treats anybody with respect, he's an idiot. These guys are all bitches -

Nate Dogg: Well, the next time you see Kurupt you ask him about it. I don't have anything to say about Kurupt or none of that old stuff. What I do have something to say about is 213 got an album out, and it's bangin'. I refuse to be a part of any of that talking shit about anybody. Kurupt said how he felt, there it is.

What's Kurupt's problem?

Snoop Dogg: Hmmm.

Why is he spouting all these things about you in magazines?

Snoop Dogg: I don't know, man. You know, the Devil works hard when you're doing God's work and, um, I wanna be doing what's right now. I can't worry about who don't like me and what they got bad to say about me. I gotta keep bein' me, and doin' what Snoop Dogg do to make the world love me and, you know, keep turnin' it out, doin' what I do. If I start focusing on them, I'm a start just sounding like them and feelin' like them and lookin' like them, and that's when I'm doin' bad. You know, they tryin' to get me to fall to they level.

Will the third Eastsidaz album ever see the light of day?

Snoop Dogg: That, I don't know. The Eastsidaz gotta come back together to do some brainstormin' amongst themselves as individuals to get they shit together and then, once they get they shit together if a third CD is possible. Hopefully, they'll do it together, on they own, or, whatever, whatever.

CHAPTER 6

IRAQ

Do you follow the news?

Snoop Dogg: Yeah, why? What's happenin'?

A lot of things. But the question is when are we going to hear the political side of Snoop Dogg?

Snoop Dogg: I don't know.

Are you at all interested in bringing that Chuck D flava?

Snoop Dogg: I dunno, man. I used to like Public Enemy as a kid, but I never thought that I could even rap that style, be tryin' to give messages and shit. I just try to speak my mind, but at the same time people get the message that I'm bringing, and they know I stand for what's right, and what's real.

What about Nate Dogg and Warren G doing something like Harold Melvin & The Bluenotes? A political message for the times. You have a lot of ears open.

Nate Dogg: Right now I'm not a politician. My job is to make music that people love and to make sure that my kids have a nice little stack of change when I'm not here.

So right now I'm trying to secure my future, and then I might get into politics. But that's not my job right now. My job is to make music. I make music to make people happy. Please get your mind off of politics. Listen to some Nate Dogg music. I do have a message – get out and vote. I don't have any other political message nor any other agenda, just if you believe in something go vote.

Any thoughts on George W. Bush?

Snoop Dogg: I don't have any thoughts. You know he's the President, I ain't gonna slander him or talk bad about him.

What's your opinion on the situation in Iraq?

Snoop Dogg: Man, I don't know. I try not to focus on all that. I'm just tryin' to make records and handle my business right now.

What do you think of George W. Bush and the war in Iraq?

Bishop Don Magic Juan: Man, I'm like the rest of Americans and foreigners and everybody else. I think it's a tragic thing and there's so much tragedy when it's close to home. Some of your fathers or your sisters or your brothers get killed. But like I say, the Bible says 'Render the season what they'll give to God was his'.

President Bush, the leader of the United States and we have to follow. Chuuch! Got to run now. Got to go off and take care of God's business. The Archbishop Don Magic Juan, Chairman of the Board of famous players everywhere! Preach Tabernacle Chuuch!

What do you think of the war in Iraq and Afghanistan?

Nate Dogg: I think we should have Bush move back to Texas. That's all I can tell you. We took our anger and did what everybody does, and we shouldn't do that. We got mad, and we struck at somebody, and I say we because we could have stopped that, but we were so mad as Americans we just let it go, like, forget it, he gonna do it anyway. We struck at the first person there. We didn't hit who we should have hit. True enough, Saddam wasn't shit. But that ain't our job. So, if Saddam thought Bush wasn't shit, which he ain't, what if he came over here and took Bush out of office? That was never gonna happen. We started something we'll never be able to end now. That's what I think.

What do you think of the whole gun mentality America has?

Nate Dogg: Shit, I think we better keep that motherfucking mentality now because we done started some shit. It's a bad mentality to have, but we are at war now, so it's a smart mentality to have now. We've been pushed into a fight now by one person or by the situation around this whole thing. We're in it now.

CHAPTER 7

WIN ONE SOON

In between solo albums, collabos, guest drops, and recording the new 213 album, Nate Dogg finds time to squeeze in a little court-side action with **NBA Live**. With so much wisdom to offer in his own game, we asked the MVP to fill in some dots with that other game.

***

Who is your team on NBA Live?

Nate Dogg: *NBA Live* my team is Dallas because Nowitzki never misses a three, which brings me to another subject - what the fuck is wrong with the Lakers? They fittin' to hire me too next week? Did you all hear who they hired as the Head Coach? They hired him twenty minutes ago, a Japanese dude. He's called Win One Soon. He's tight.

What's wrong with the Lakers?

Nate Dogg: They just need chemistry. They forced chemistry together, and it wasn't the right one. If you play basketball, you have to understand if the chemistry is not there you'll never win. The chemistry was never there. They were winning off pure talent alone. And then when it came down to a team that was all about defence and clicking, the defense brought about Detroit's offence. You can't even really pick an MVP off of Detroit. The whole team just whopped our ass. If they had said, the whole team is MVP I wouldn't have been mad at all.

What's your take on the Eastern Conference?

Nate Dogg: Right now, it's cool to me. Before the season started every last one of us out here said somebody from the West gonna win it. I'm through being sceptical and guessing what's gonna happen because I don't know. I know basketball, but you don't know people's hearts. Rasheed Wallace was on three teams last season. The last one he got to he ended up being a world champion. He stopped in Atlanta for a cup of coffee and kept on going. He's Rasheed; he can play ball. I'm surprised they clicked in with him, but he went down there and ended up bringing up something out of them.

What do you do with your free time?

Snoop Dogg: Play *Madden*.

CHAPTER 8

THE REAL NATE DOGG

What do you bring to the table that makes Nate Dogg so hot?

Nate Dogg: I'm just Nate, my voice. I can't take credit for that. I was born with a voice and when I put it on music people like it and that's all. I just keep putting it on music until they don't like it.

Where do you feel you are at this stage?

Nate Dogg: I'm in a beautiful place in this stage, man. Not only do I have a record deal, but I can also do side-order deals, and everybody wants me to be on their record. I'm in a great place right now. I can remember twelve years ago when I was running behind Dr Dre begging to get on a song, and now it's people calling me to be on a song.

I got one double and one single Nate Dogg's Greatest Hits alone.

Nate Dogg: I went to the swap meet and got one. I was mad at 'em, but they had it, so I went and got it. I had to do it. I think it was, like, thirty songs on there. It wasn't any of the recent songs. I'm just trying to work, man, that's what I'm trying to do.

Who would you compare yourself to as a back in the day soul singer? If R. Kelly is Donny Hathaway, who is Nate Dogg?

Nate Dogg: R. Kelly is Donny Hathaway? I didn't know that. Marvin Gaye O'Brien type. Marvin Gaye was the soulful singer with messages in his music. He went everywhere with his music, so yeah.

What do you think of the R&B right now?

Nate Dogg: It's cool. I don't think it's up to par. I think we need somebody soulful. I mean, with a soulful voice and singing about soulful stuff. It's different. Like, right now, everybody's singing about sex, like things I sing. I'm not like an R&B singer like that. But, you know, people be one song they got is about sex, the next one is about weed or something because it's the sign of the times. But I think R&B singers should be like R&B to me, like on some old love shit. Like Marvin Gaye's "Sexual Healing," them kind of songs. Or Earth Wind & Fire's, "That's The Way of the World." Where them kind of things? Where them songs went? Those are the kind of songs that I'm looking for that I haven't heard in years.

Warren G: Kanye West.

Nate Dogg: Kanye West is a rapper, though. He tight as fuck, which brings me to Kanye West. He's one of the tightest cats on earth right now. When it comes to his skills and his production, the way he put his album together is a masterpiece. He should win every rap award this year.

Where do you feel you are in the history of the last ten years of Hip-Hop?

Nate Dogg: I don't know. My daddy told me once, 'Don't ever praise yourself. Let somebody else praise you'. You got to ask the public. Ask the people where I am, and I guess they'll tell you and I guess I'll know too.

CHAPTER 9

THE REAL SNOOP DOGG

No one can deny Snoop Dogg is one of the most recognisable figures in pop culture. Did you ever expect to break through like this?

Snoop Dogg: Nah, not really. You can't expect that. You just wanna get in where you fit in and be heard and seen. That's all it was about for me in the beginning, just being heard. You know, wanting people to respect what I do and how I do it.

What makes people relate to Snoop Dogg?

Snoop Dogg: That, I don't know. You know, it's hard to tell but, at the same time, I'm enjoyin' it.

When people look back on your place in history, what are they going to think?

Snoop Dogg: I don't know what people gonna think. I think that I did a good job. I still got work to do, but at the same time, I'm doin' me.

What do you love about Canada?

Snoop Dogg: The bitches and the weed.

Any last words?

Snoop Dogg: Stay down with Snoop Dogg, I'm a be here for fifty more years.

CHAPTER 10

THE REAL BISHOP DON MAGIC JUAN

Jesus, he ain't. But if Luke 8:3 is any indication, Archbishop Don Magic Juan isn't the first one to have preached off the avails of women.

***

What's on your mind these days?

Bishop Don Magic Juan: Well, Jesus always on my mind. Right now, I'm going through some things as far as movies, recordings, a clothing line, got an action figure doll coming out. Some great things is happening. Hanging out with Snoop Dogg. We continue to do things, stepping up our game in this new macking millennium, you dig? We are bringing it on now. Ain't no time to waste and ain't no sense in playing. Recess is over. Players got to step their game up and go and do whatever it is they got to do to make it happen. Tomorrow is not promised. You got to do what you can today. You can't put it off 'til tomorrow. That's what's going on in my life. I'm doing everything that I can be blessed to do. I'm honoured to be flying around the country hosting Player Ball. I just finished shooting a video with Eightball and MJG, "Cadillac Pimping." It be coming out soon. It's a Bad Boy production. P. Diddy called me and asked me would I do it. Definitely, for him, it's a-okay.

Describe the Bishop style.

Bishop Don Magic Juan: Oh, one of a kind. Green for the money, gold for the honey. Being suited and booted from head to toe. Matching pieces. The shoes look like the suit; the suit looks like the shirt, the shirt looks like the hat. It's going down player. I'm the real deal. I got thirty years in this game. I ain't missed a day without checking paper from a female. They know I'm the real bling blinger. It ain't no joke. I'm glad to have this opportunity to be travelling with Snoop Dogg, being his spiritual advisor, having a chance to counsel him on different issues of life that he's going through that I can share with him from my old school experience. So it's happening.

I spoke with a man named Scoop Jackson.

Bishop Don Magic Juan: Scoop a good friend of mine.

He told me you're like a father to him.

Bishop Don Magic Juan: I've been knowing him since he started off in the journalist field and everything, and I'm proud to say I'm a friend of his and I like where writing has taken him. It's taken him and his family to greater heights, and that's a blessing. I pray for people all over the world. That's what we all need to do: love one another, and I tell people, if you want somebody to treat you right, you treat them right. You just show them how you treat them and they'll treat you the same way.

What about these new school pimps? Are they doing it right?

Bishop Don Magic Juan: They are definitely not doing it right, but you know everybody entitled to a shot at the game. If you don't play it right, you're not gonna make it no way. People are happy with the word 'pimp' now. It seems to be a very popular thing to say for a lot of people, and it's just bringing joy and making people feel more respective about the dressing and everything. It's a good thing as long as it happens. I never thought it'd come this far.

I read Pimping Ken claim you are using the word 'Jesus' in vain.

Bishop Don Magic Juan: Well, one thing about it Ken don't know. I was through with the game before he even started in the game, and I don't think he ever reached the level, and he could never get to the level of the game that I play. So a lot of things that I'm doing and will be doing is gonna be a mystery to him because he is not familiar with this real true game. He's definitely a friend, and what I'm saying is he misconstrued. He don't understand he's supposed to ask me. I'm the Chairman of the Board, so 'church' means just like anything else, like saying God bless you. So for those that don't know and think we are playing with the word 'church', 'church' is like saying God bless you. You can't get a lot of players or hardcore pimps and hustlers to say God bless you, but you can get 'em to say 'church'. If anybody's spiritual - and some of the people don't even go to church, know better that the Bible said that we are the church and Jesus is the head of the church. When we are saying 'church' we right in the line of what the Lord wants us to say. So to Kenny Ivey, hey, just watch me. Follow me. I'm the leader. I know this game. I got thirty years plus experience. You probably ain't even thirty yet. Chuuch! And that's from the Archbishop Don Magic Juan. Now run tell that!

Who elected you Chairman of the Board?

Bishop Don Magic Juan: Famous players all over the world. That means Big Snoop Dogg. That means all the pimps and players and hustlers around the country. I'm recognised for my style, for my experience, for my quality, for the game I share with others. With the stuff I use ain't no player ever lost. I know the game, man, and that ain't no joke. Chuuuch!

Chapter 11

GROUPIE LUV

WAIT, WAIT, WAIT. THERE'S MORE? Here is a beautiful selection of behind the scenes photos taken while Rob Harris and I waited for our interviews. Sadly, we were not able to connect with Snoop Dogg this day. However, it could have been much worse. The scenery was out of the world!

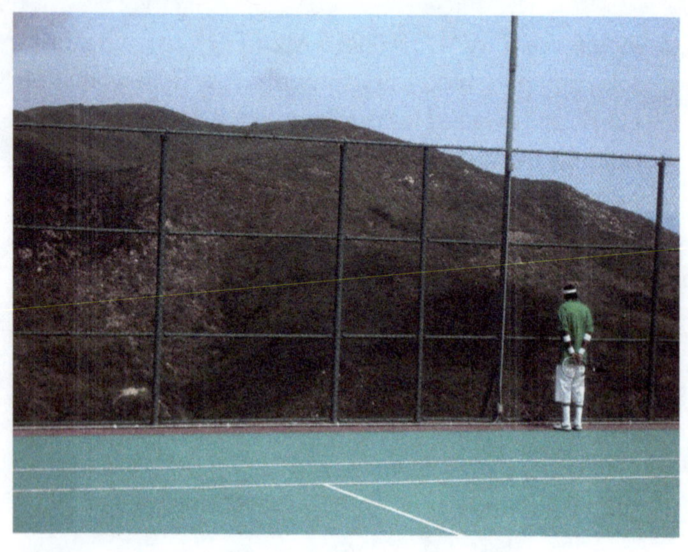

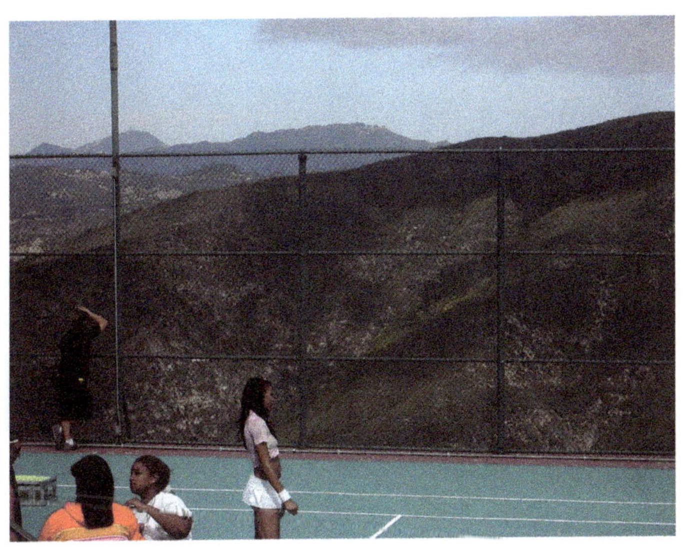

This is not Serena or Venus

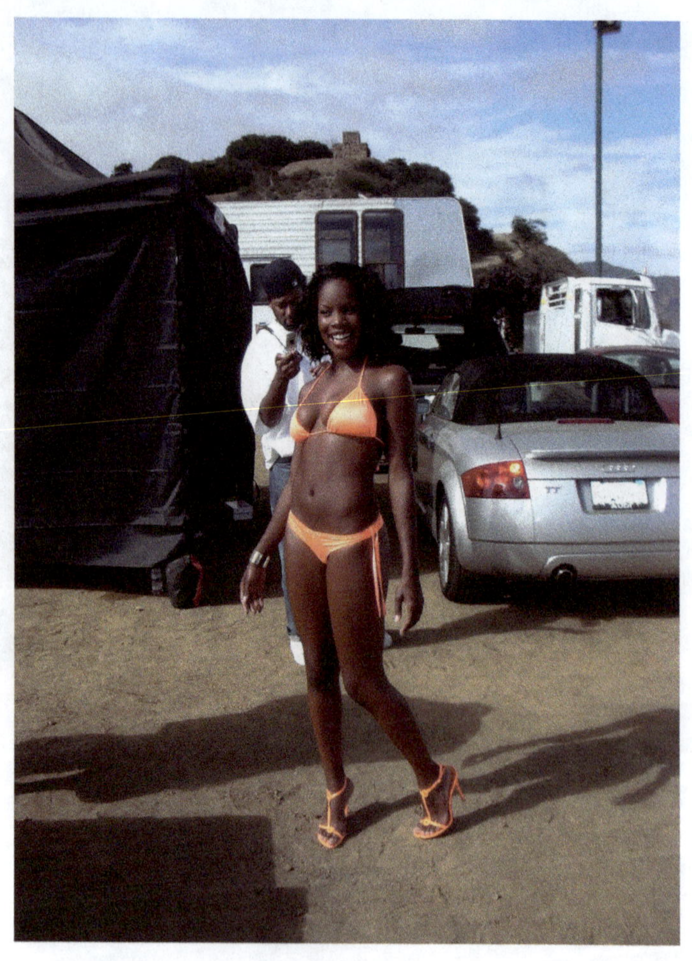

A wonderful smile

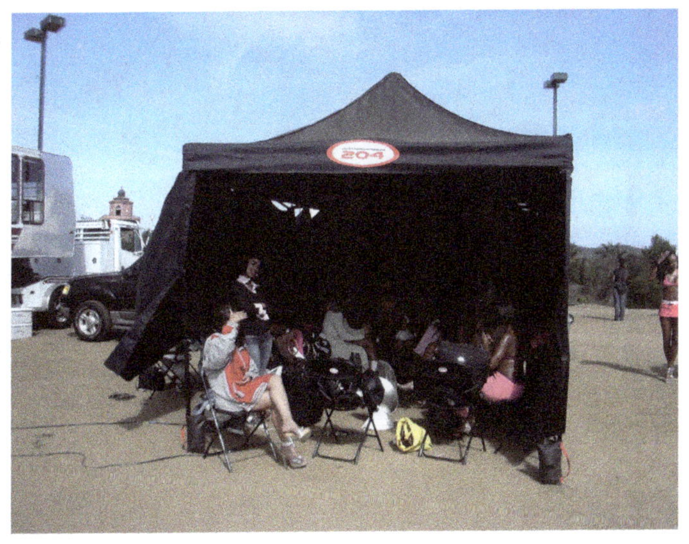

Waiting for a girl like you

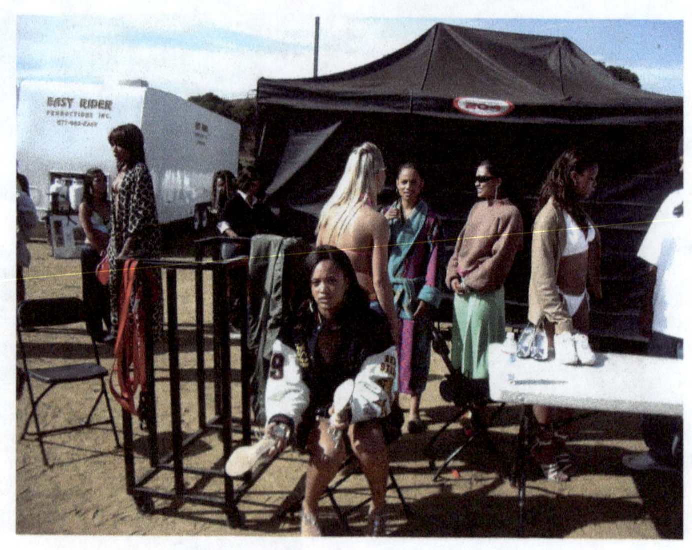

Fly swatter

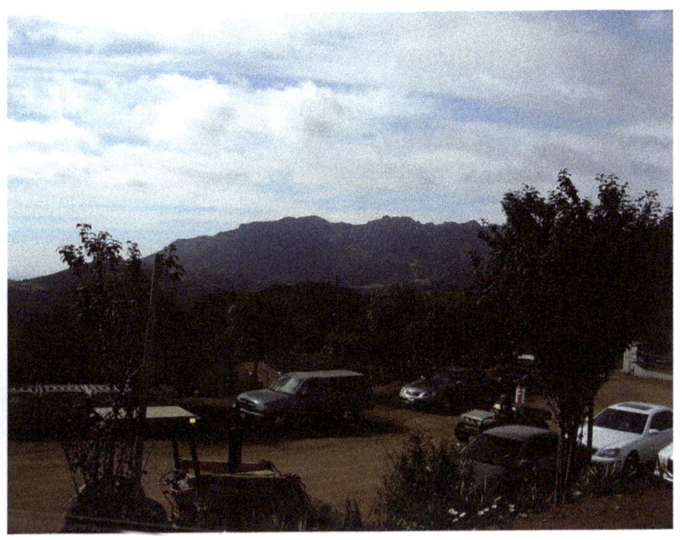

Top of the world, ma

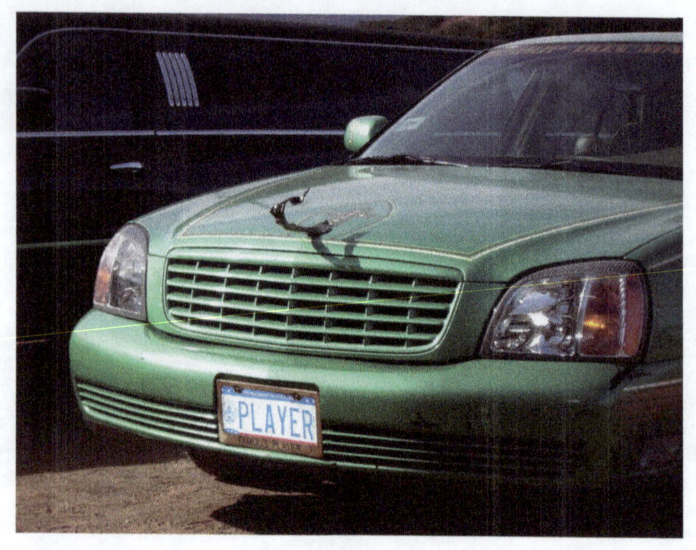

Guess who drives this car?

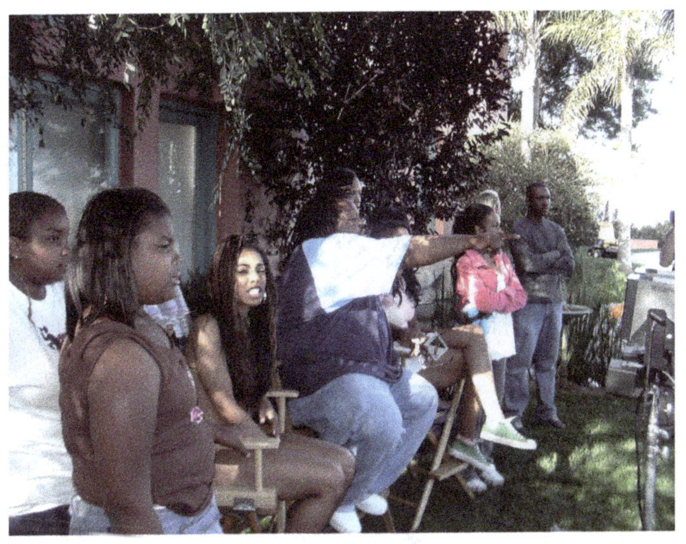

Director Chris Robinson points the way

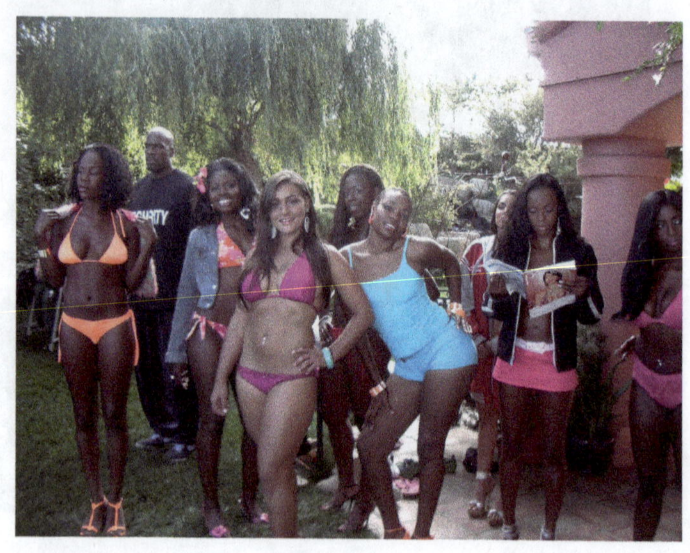

The stars of "Groupie Luv"

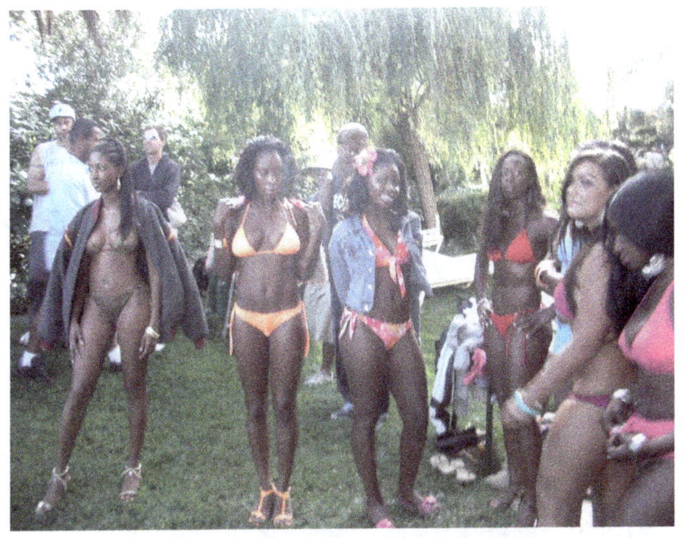

Today is a good day!

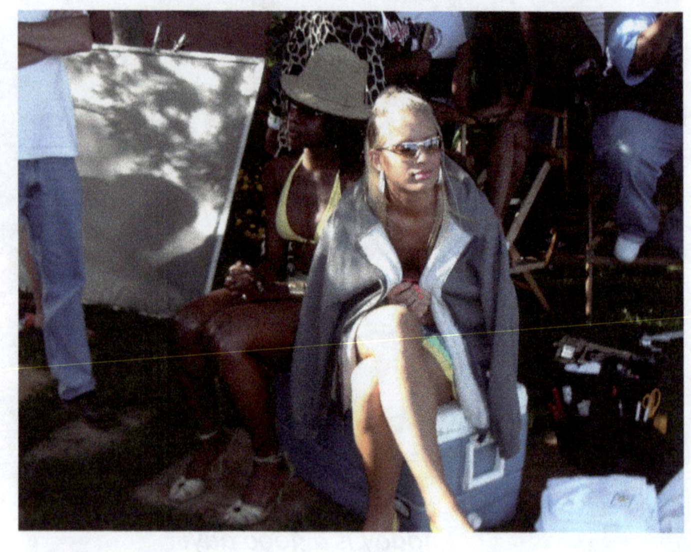

What's in the cooler?

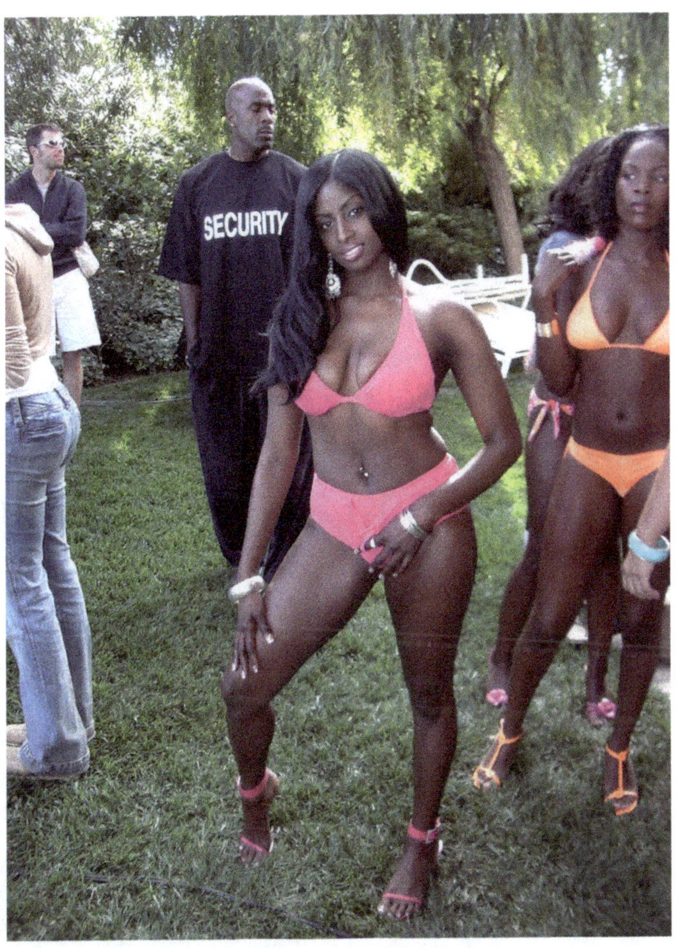

It's real serious up here

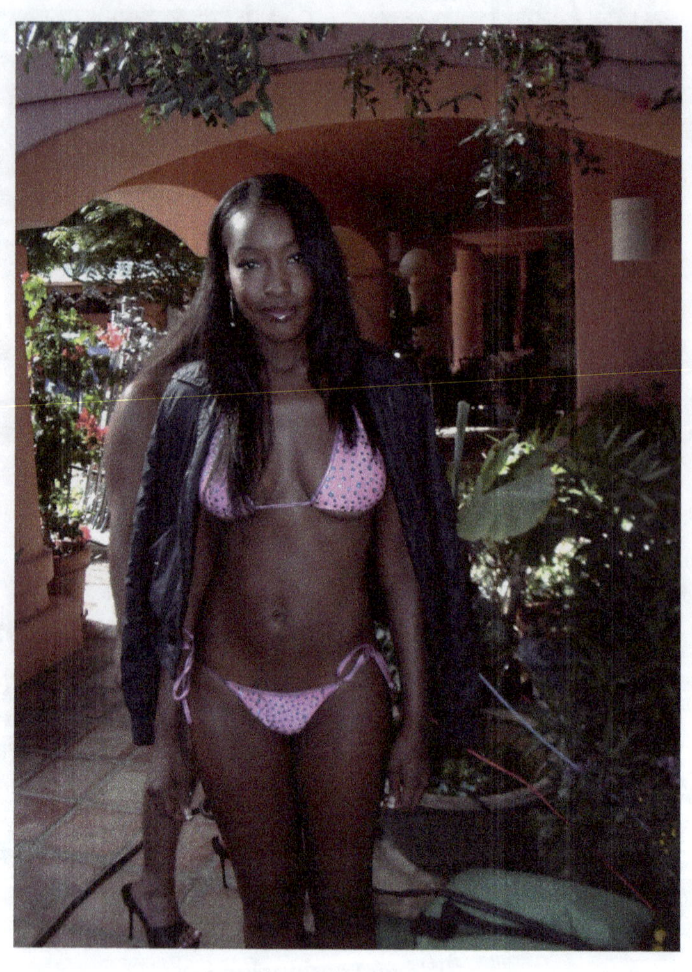

Perfection!

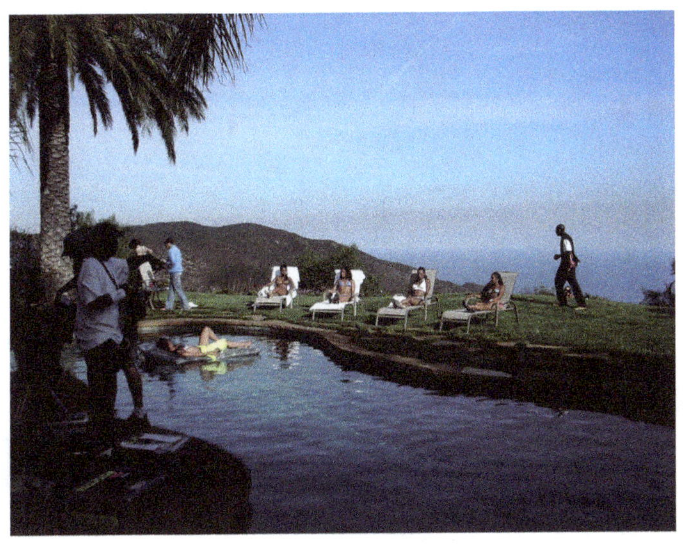

Poolside

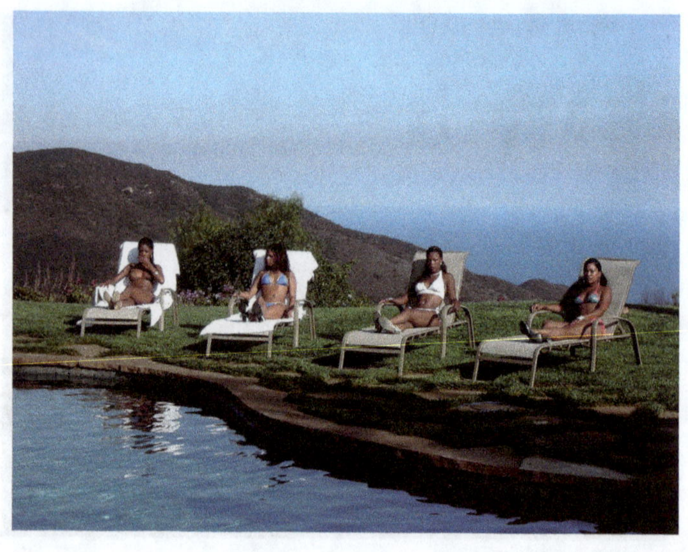

Still here by the pool overlooking the mountains

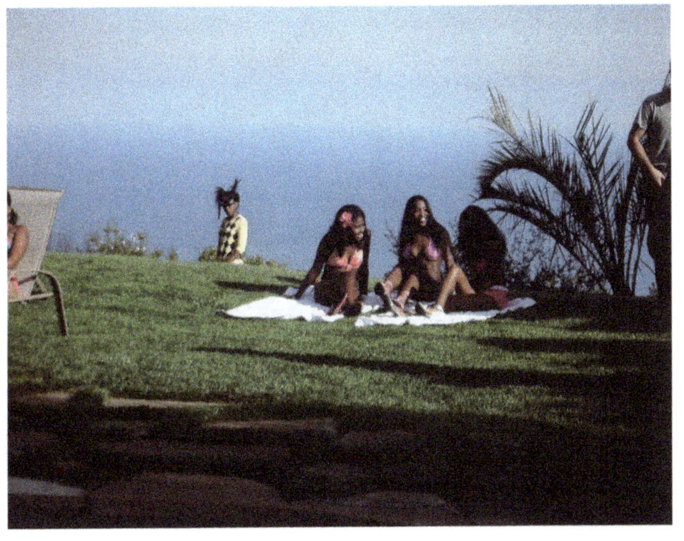

Smiling and profiling

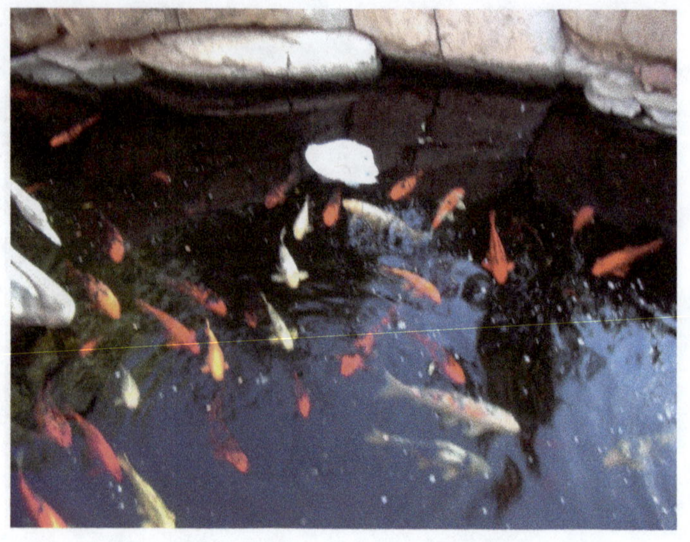

Wish I had a Koi pond by my gates

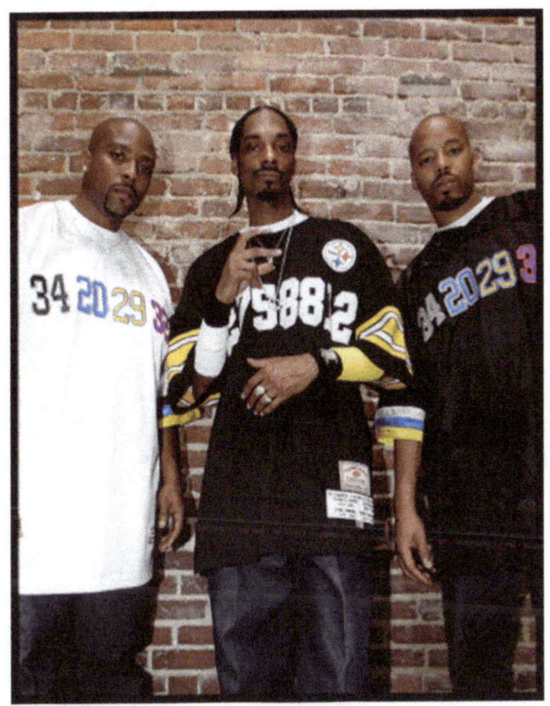

by Craig Boyko

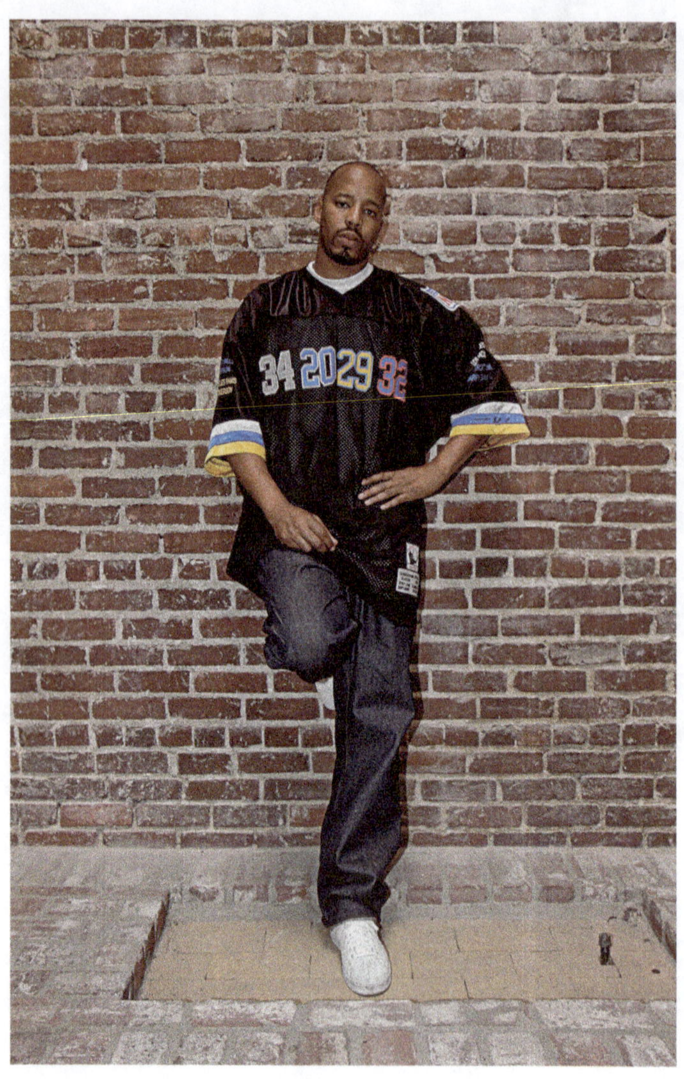

by Craig Boyko

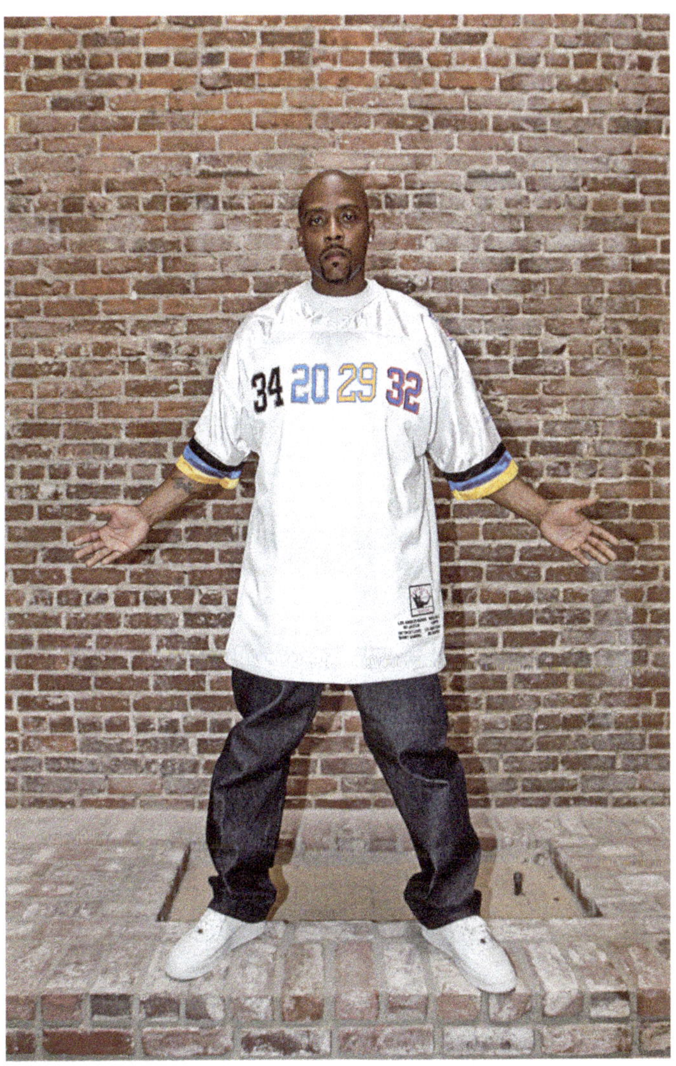

by Craig Boyko

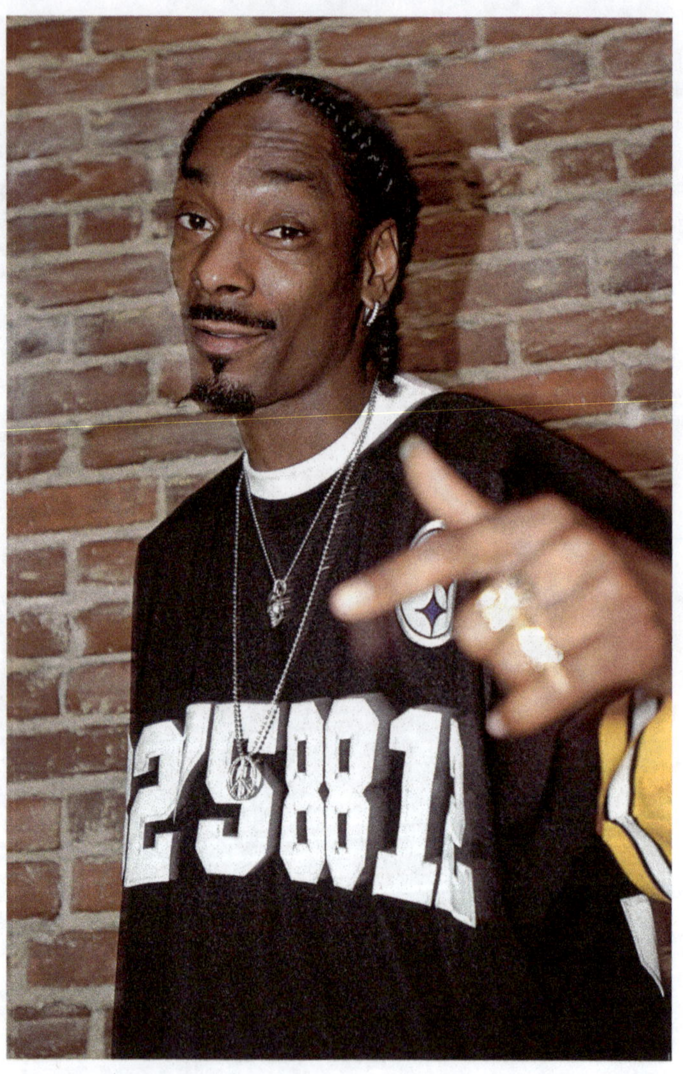

by Craig Boyko

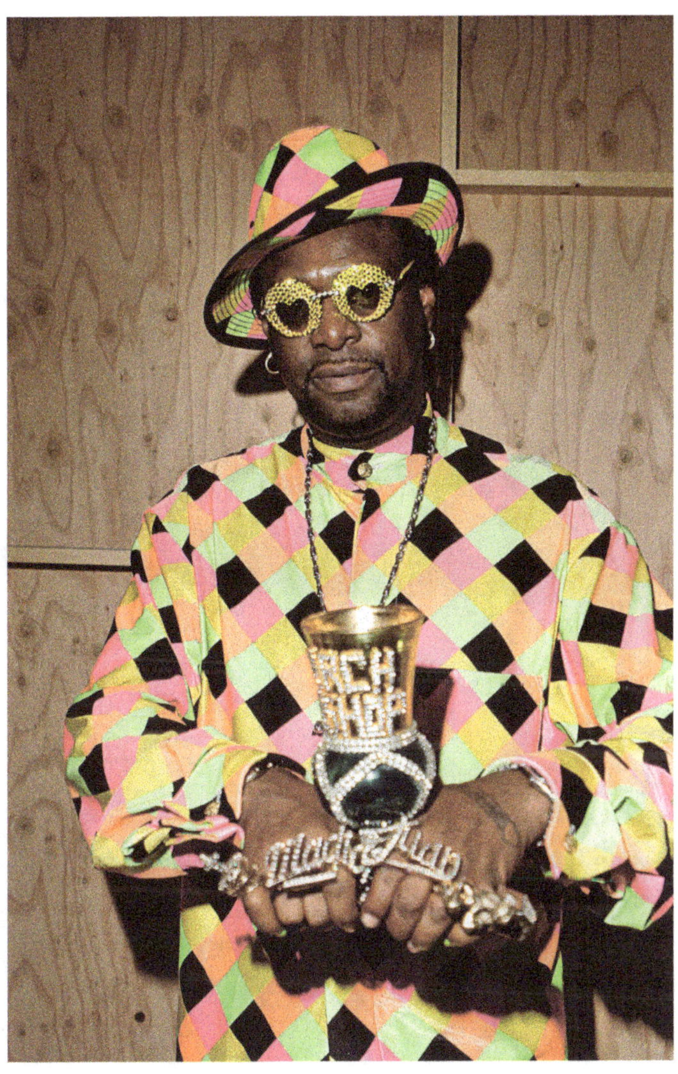

by Craig Boyko

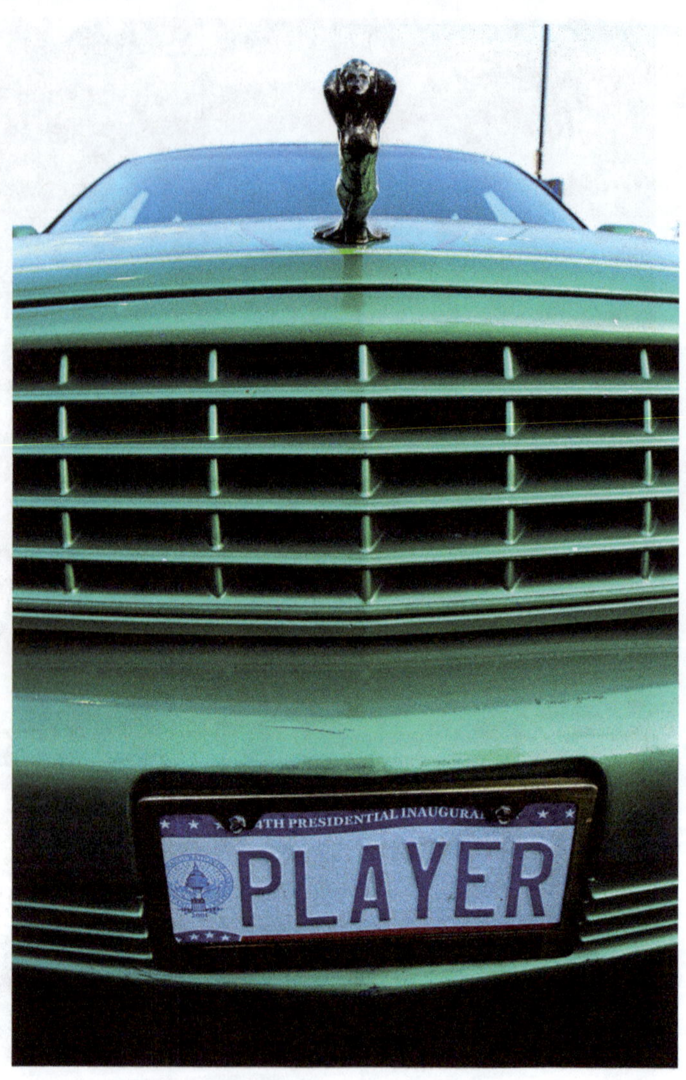

by Craig Boyko

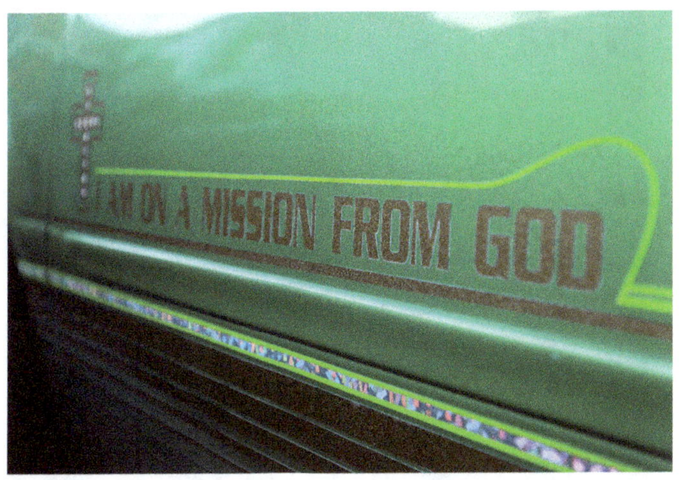

by Craig Boyko

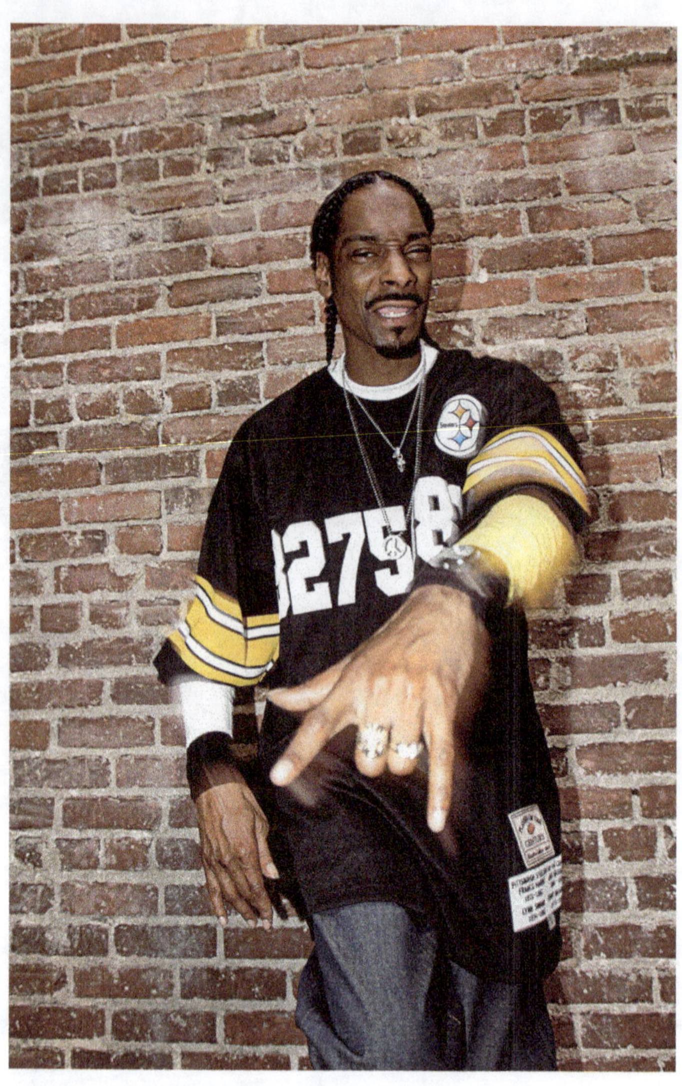

by Craig Boyko

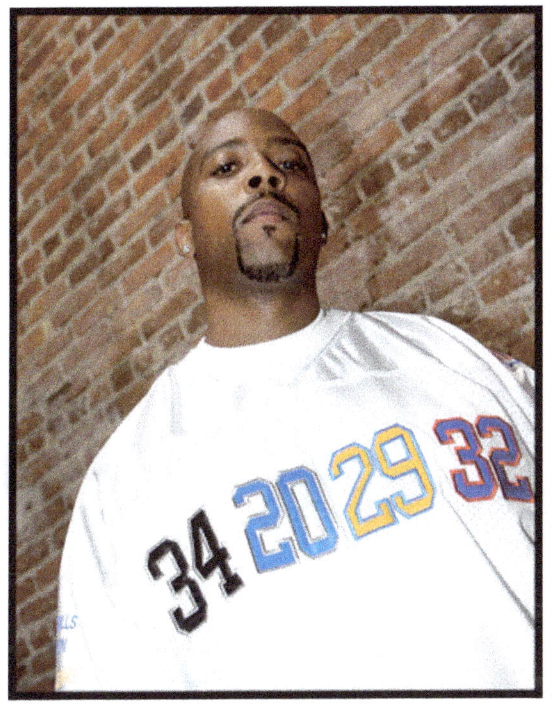

by Craig Boyko

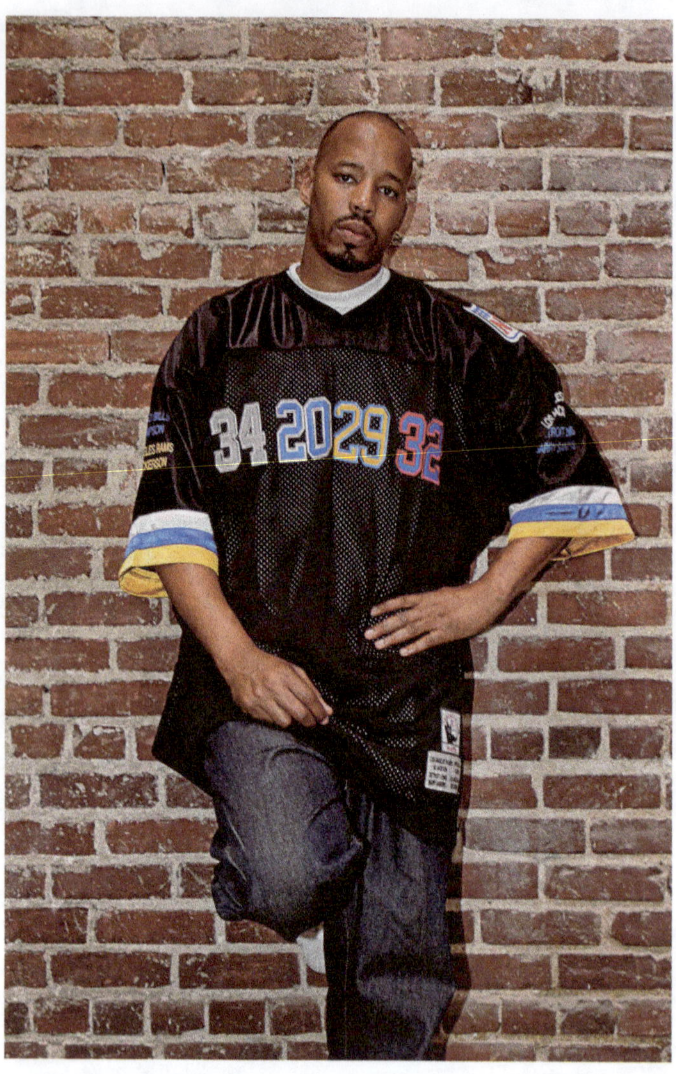

by Craig Boyko

63

DISCOGRAPHY

Albums

The Hard Way - August 17, 2004 (TVT/Doggystyle)

Videos

"So Fly" (2003)

"Groupie Luv" (2004)

Guest Appearances

"Deeez Nuuuts" Dr. Dre The Chronic 213 with Dr. Dre & Daz Dillinger (1992)

"Ain't No Fun (If the Homies Can't Have None)" Snoop Doggy Dogg Doggystyle 213 with Nanci Fletcher and Kurupt (1993)

"Groupie" Snoop Doggy Dogg Tha Doggfather 213 with Tha Dogg Pound and Charlie Wilson (1996)

"Friends" Nate Dogg G-Funk Classics, Vol. 1 & 2 (1998)

"Neva Gonna Give It Up" Kurupt Tha Streetz Iz a Mutha with Kurupt, Soopafly and Tray Deee (1999)

"Don't Tell" Snoop Dogg No Limit Top Dogg 213 with Mausberg (1999)

"Game Don't Wait" Warren G I Want It All (1999)

"Game Don't Wait (Remix)" Warren G I Want It All 213 with Xzibit (1999)

"Can't Go For That (Remix)" Tamia A Nu Day (2000)

"Yo' Sassy Ways" Warren G The Return of the Regulator (2001)

"From Long Beach 2 Brick City" Snoop Dogg Paid Tha Cost To Be Da Boss 213 with Redman (2002)

"Family Reunion" DPG: The Unreleased Collection 213 with Badd Azz and Soopafly (2003)

"Rollin' Down The Highway" Snoop Dogg Welcome To Tha Chuuch Volume 9 "Run Tell Dat" 213 with Tray Dee (2004)

"PYT" Warren G In the Mid-Nite Hour (2005)

ABOUT THE AUTHOR

Father. Son. Brother.

HARRIS ROSEN was born and lives in Toronto, Canada. He is the force and Author of the Behind The Music Tales series. His book **N.W.A: *The Aftermath*** was #1 on Amazon in the United States, Canada, France, Australia and Japan!

For twenty years, he self-published the national lifestyle magazine Peace! He has interviewed hundreds of composers, artists, actors and athletes, including the Notorious B.I.G., Dr. Dre, Daft Punk, Eminem, Derek Jeter, Georges St. Pierre, Nirvana, Metallica, Chris Rock, Buju Banton, Beastie Boys, Kiss, Destiny's Child and Aaliyah to list a few.

He has gone to six continents and was in the midst of a whirlwind of multiple musical cultural revolutions that occurred throughout the 90's and 2000s, while compiling a true and honest archive of audio, images and video.

behindthemusictales.com
facebook.com/behindthemusictales
instagram.com/behindthemusictales
twitter.com/mrheller1

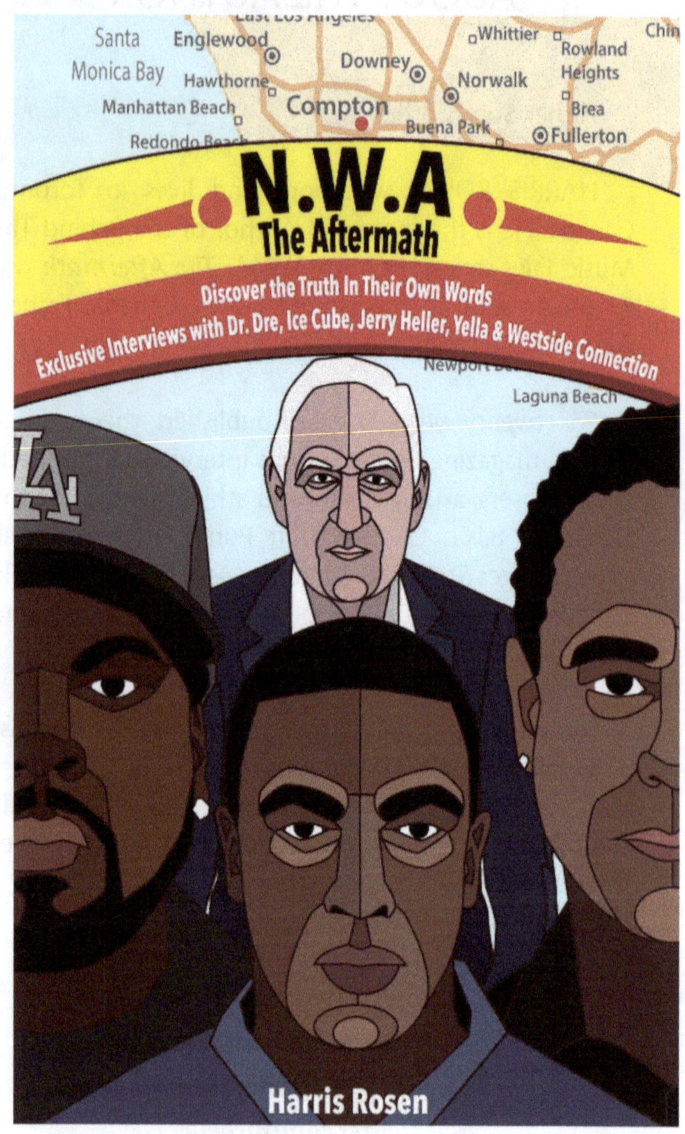
Santa Monica Bay
Englewood
East Los Angeles
Whittier
Chin
Rowland Heights
Hawthorne
Downey
Norwalk
Manhattan Beach
Compton
Brea
Redondo Beach
Buena Park
Fullerton
N.W.A
The Aftermath
Discover the Truth In Their Own Words
Exclusive Interviews with Dr. Dre, Ice Cube, Jerry Heller, Yella & Westside Connection
Newport
Laguna Beach
LA
Harris Rosen

[N.W.A Fans Only!] Astonishing facts revealed for the first time!

DR. DRE: *Tupac never knew me.*

ICE CUBE: *I just do shit for Ice Cube fans, not for Hip-Hop fans.*

YELLA: *Me and Dre produced all Eazy, N.W.A. All of that. Me and him did that together.*

JERRY HELLER: *There are people that think that I am the white Devil.*

N.W.A: The Aftermath is your one-way ticket deep inside the world's most dangerous group. It will blow your mind!

Others have sensationalised much of what you will read here in a manner of journalistic psycho-speak. **N.W.A: The Aftermath** is as close to the truth as one can get. It delivers raw thoughts by real people and is manifested directly in the voice and words of the artists who made it happen.

Each chapter will unravel tall tales and give you new insight. Don't miss out on the opportunity to learn what happened.

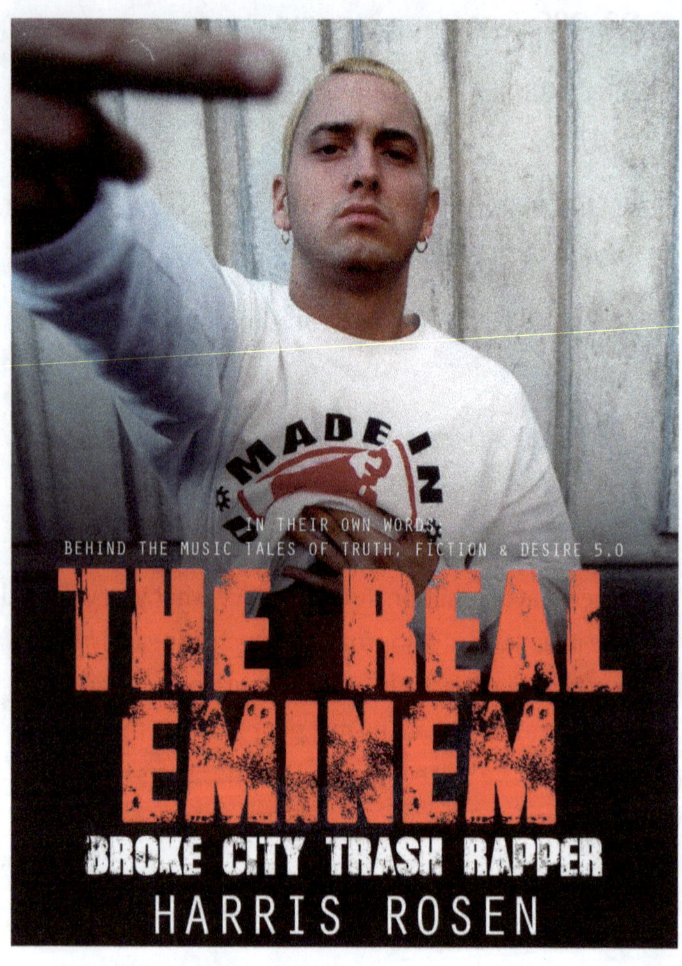
IN THEIR OWN WORDS:
BEHIND THE MUSIC TALES OF TRUTH, FICTION & DESIRE 5.0
THE REAL EMINEM
BROKE CITY TRASH RAPPER
HARRIS ROSEN

Exclusive audio, rare unreleased songs and interviews with Eminem & D12.

The Real Eminem: Broke City Trash Rapper is your one-way ticket deep inside the mind of the real Eminem. It will blow your mind!

This book contains two exclusive in-person April 1999 interviews with Eminem and one exclusive in-person 2001 interview with D12.

These exclusive, original interviews deliver a hard twenty-six-year-old Eminem, the real Eminem as an angry young man eager to prove himself to the world and give them the middle-finger at the same time. These interviews deliver an Eminem solely concerned with representing himself, his family, and those he came up with in his time of need. These conversations provide an Eminem who proudly declared he lived for the day.

Eminem didn't invent ill rhyming or the ill lower class mentality. However, he had lived it, seen it, done it, and was now speaking on it for the world to hear. Eminem was not a bad guy. Everything he wrote, rapped or expressed had been in the mix, in one form or another, before.

The second part of the book features an exclusive 2001 interview with D12. It provides a first-hand look into the "Just Don't Give A Fuck" mindset of the crew and choice background information on Eminem in the midst of becoming an international phenomenon.

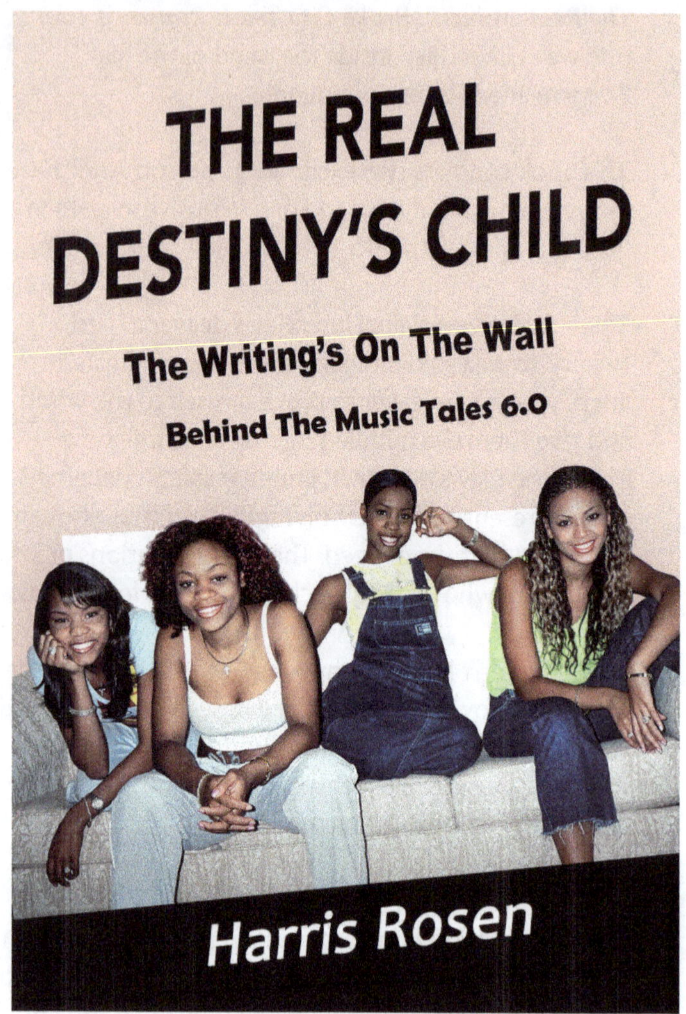
THE REAL
DESTINY'S CHILD
The Writing's On The Wall
Behind The Music Tales 6.0
Harris Rosen

An intimate portrait of Destiny's Child and the girl who would be Queen.

A revealing eye on the state of the union of The Real Destiny's Child in the months leading up to their bitter separation. Never before heard revelations leading up to the inconceivable truth.

The Real Destiny's Child captures Destiny's Child at the most pivotal time in their career. This book is straight talk direct from the group in their own words. A rare opportunity to go deep Behind The Music Tales and inside their minds documenting **The Writing's On The Wall** album, love, hope, dreams and more.

In these pages you'll discover:

- **EXCLUSIVE** spring 1999 casual photo shoot with Beyonce, Kelly, LeToya & LaTavia
- **EXCLUSIVE** prints from the **Bootylicious Remix video**
- **EXCLUSIVE** song-by-song breakdown of **The Writing's on the Wall** by Beyonce, Kelly, LeToya & LaTavia
- Rare pre-teen video auditions, rehearsals and unreleased songs

Many people know Destiny's Child as one of the most successful groups of all time. Then at the height of their popularity, they broke up. Here they are revealing their struggles for fame and love mere months before the descent and madness.

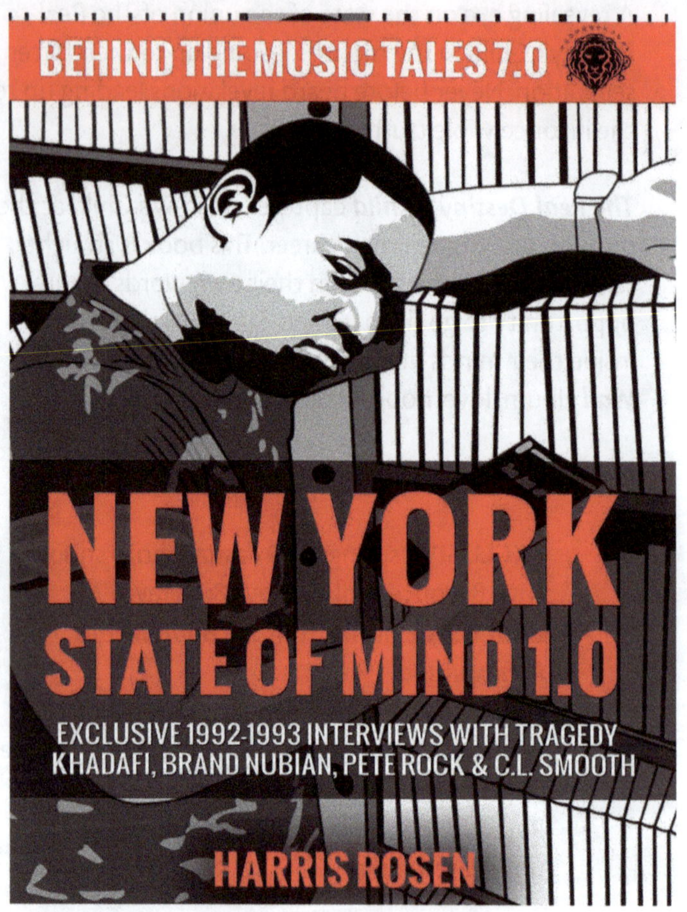
BEHIND THE MUSIC TALES 7.0
NEW YORK
STATE OF MIND 1.0
EXCLUSIVE 1992-1993 INTERVIEWS WITH TRAGEDY
KHADAFI, BRAND NUBIAN, PETE ROCK & C.L. SMOOTH
HARRIS ROSEN

A fascinating genuine narrative formed in the crucible of Golden Age Hip-Hop mindfulness.

New York State of Mind 1.0, the 7th book in the series, provides you with an authentic flavour of the personalities, in all their raw forms, who breathed life into the streets of the city, taking the music to new heights and in entirely new directions.

Tragedy Khadafi is as real as it gets. Through impressive MC skills and a formidable street reputation, he lived the life of a real hoodlum, surviving gunshot wounds, stabbings and broken bones. The strong lyrical message of Brand Nubian reflects on the group's identity as Five-Percenters and the philosophy of the Nation of Gods and Earth, while Pete Rock & C.L. Smooth arrived on the scene in the midst of a Hip-Hop impasse of sorts.

New York State of Mind 1.0 is a candid look deep inside the psyche of each and an examination of what makes them tick. Take a ride alongside them and learn how they made their mark on a generation.

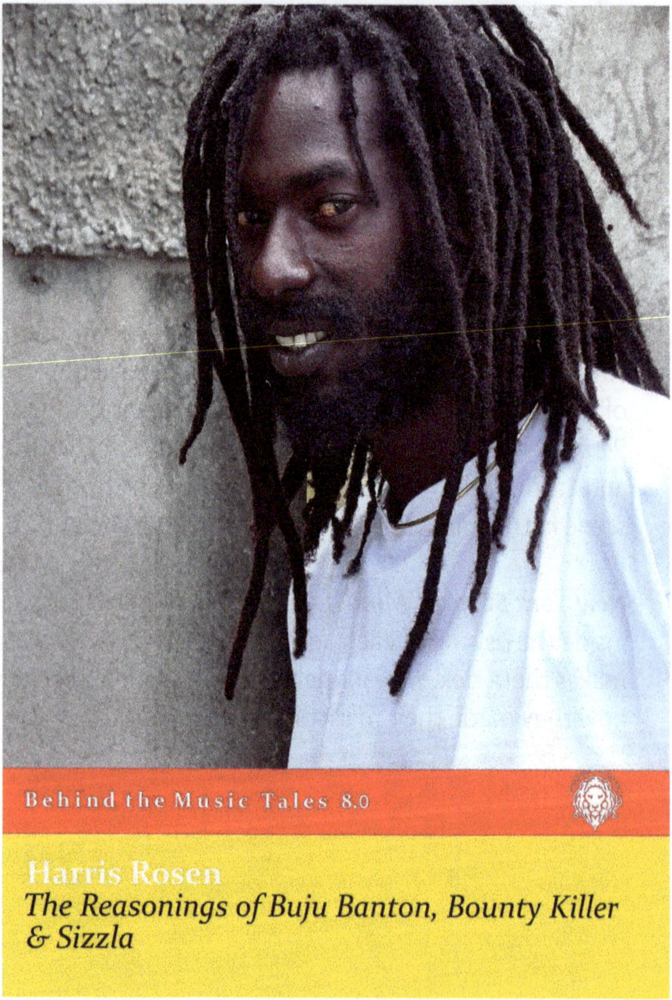

Behind the Music Tales 8.0
Harris Rosen
The Reasonings of Buju Banton, Bounty Killer
& Sizzla

An engaging literal account of how three prodigious talents ply and impact a nation of millions with their reactionary music.

Now, in *The Reasonings of Buju Banton, Bounty Killer & Sizzla*, the 8th book in the series, you can get inside the minds of some of the most important artists who have made their mark on Reggae music for generations to come.

Buju Banton is one of these men. A certified natural talent, his career was hallmarked by his socio-political and overtly sexual lyrics. Then he turned his back and became a devout Rastafarian.

Bounty Killer is acknowledged far and wide as The Warlord. His commanding delivery, attitude and streetwise outlaw music made him one of the biggest stars of his generation. He has likewise spoken candidly about the state of Reggae music and what was keeping it back from crossing over to the masses. Then he faced his most formidable opponent, ever.

Sizzla has released over 60 albums and is respected worldwide for his music. He has actively engaged a youthful following with his spiritual Rastafarian teachings and lifestyle, educating them on corruption, oppression and how to uplift themselves.

The Reasonings of Buju Banton, Bounty Killer & Sizzla, is a rare treat. It captures the thoughts and hopes of artists who have made it their lives to bring one of the most popular forms of music to a much more comprehensive audience.

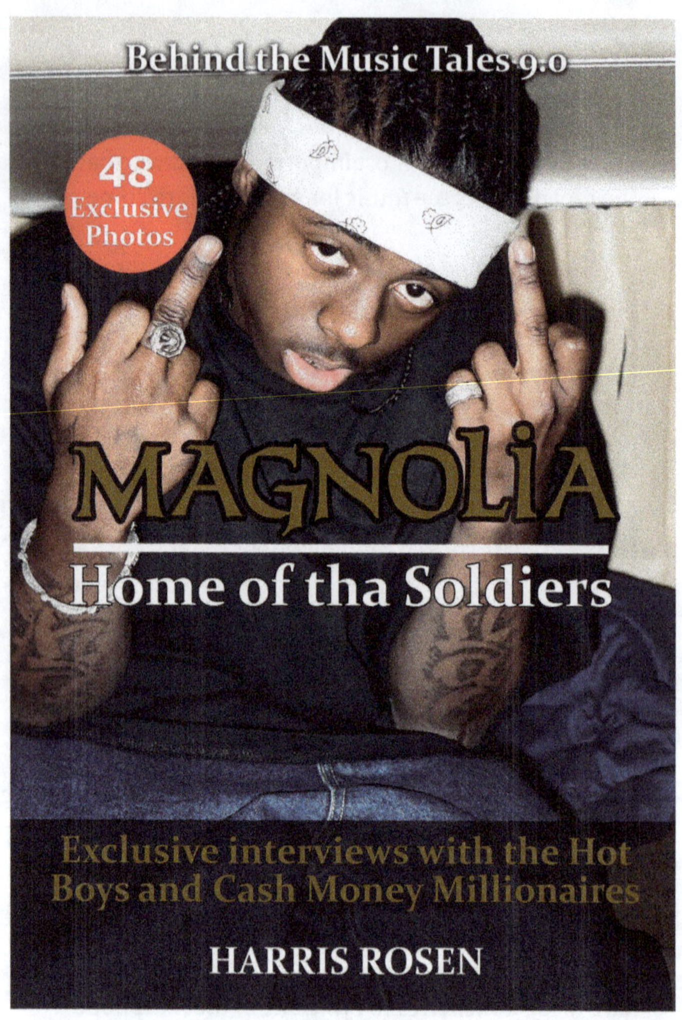
Behind the Music Tales 9.0
48 Exclusive Photos
MAGNOLIA
Home of tha Soldiers
Exclusive interviews with the Hot Boys and Cash Money Millionaires
HARRIS ROSEN

A riveting historical account of how two hustlers invested everything in one 10 years old and changed the music business, forever!

Magnolia: Home of tha Soldiers, the 9th book in the series, is a look at how Cash Money Records produced some of the iconic stars of the last two decades, and continues to cash in on the day.

Get raw and real Lil Wayne, B.G., Juvenile, and Turk revelations of their teen years. Learn how Mannie Fresh created all Cash Money Records music. Put some "respek" on Birman's name. Unmask the mystery of CEO "Slim" and discover the keys to success in an ultra rare enlightening interview.

Magnolia: Home of tha Soldiers is a very real account of being a young Black man hustling to put food on the table while fighting for his place in the music scene. It gets the answers you want, from a group of young artists who have had to fight and struggle every day to get what they wanted and to be where they are.

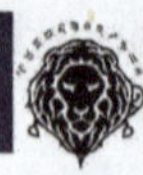

Behind The Music Tales Series (Book 11)

The Real
MC EIHT: GEAH!

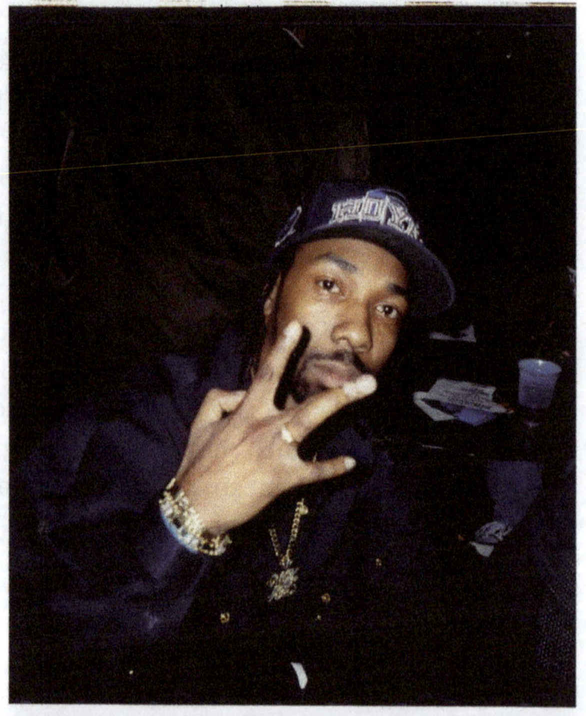

Exclusive, original interviews.
A distinct historical document.

MC Eiht = Reality Rap.

Enter the underbelly of Compton and discover the keys to success and longevity in the music game.

The Real MC Eiht: Geah!, the 11th book in the series, is more than an interview with a rapper. It's the key to building a career of longevity in the music game. By telling his story, MC Eiht reveals much about the path to success, and he does so in compelling fashion.

Stating core philosophies - of how to be a man, how to be professional, and how to give fans what they want to hear - the valuable insight, strong convictions and raw determination of MC Eiht address issues that are important to all us of, not just fans of Gangster Rap.

The Real MC Eiht: Geah! captures one of Rap's most enduring and vital artists. It is the tale of a certified foundation artist straight outta Compton, who has made his mark on Reality Rap and music for the generation to come and continues to contribute to the Art Form to this day.

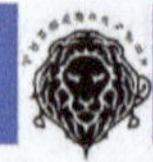

The Real
DIDDY

by Harris Rosen

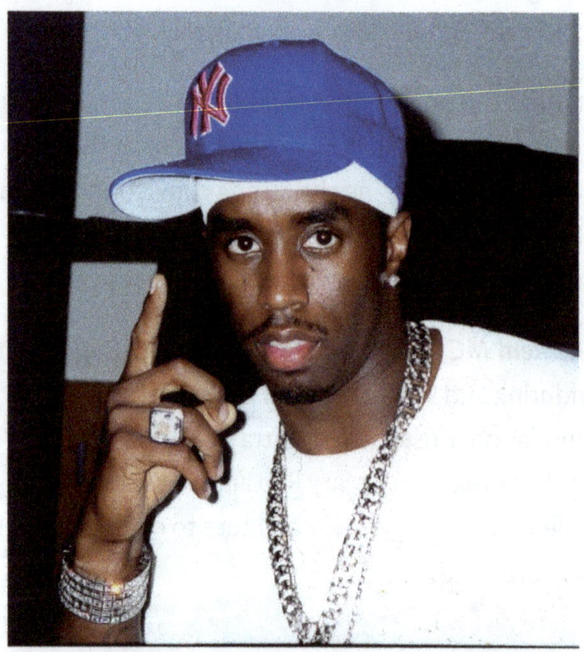

Published by Peace! Carving

Mr. Heller Press

Heller HQ

QB

Spadina-Fort York

Toronto, ON M5V 2B3

behindthemusictales.com

facebook.com/behindthemusictales

First Edition: September 2017

ISBN: 1988956013
ISBN-13: 978-1-988956-01-5
ISBN: 9780995307261 (ebook)

THE REAL 213

HARRIS ROSEN

213 photos by Craig Boyko

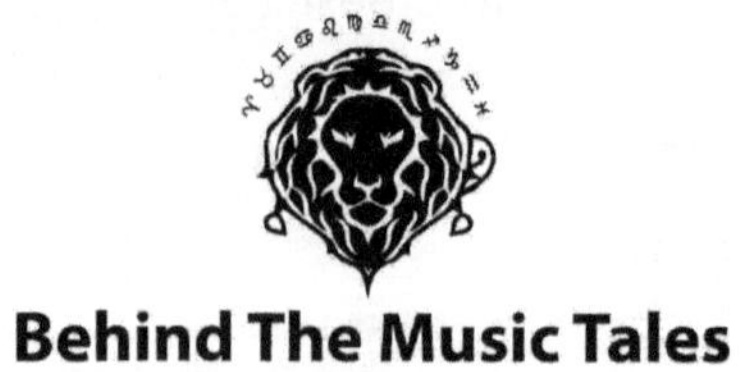

Behind The Music Tales

"This guy! I plead the fifth. This guy is nuts."
- Eminem

"Dope questions, man. Very insightful, very thoughtful."
- Guru (Gang Starr)

"You like a Psychiatrist or some shit? This shit is just coming out but go ahead."
- Mary J. Blige

"Definitely a real interview! Digging deep up in there, man. Not afraid to ask questions!"
- K-CI Hailey (Jodeci)

"The Wizard asked me for a copy of your magazine."
- Guy-Manuel de Homem-Christo (Daft Punk)

"You didn't wear your glasses, and you haven't carried your hearing aid. What else is wrong with you?"
- Bushwick Bill

"Peace and blessing, Brother Harris. Thank you for inspiring my words. Keep 'yo balance."
- Erykah Badu

"Can I see that pen?"
- Bobby Brown

"What else do you want to know? Talk to me."
- Aaliyah

Other Behind The Music Tales Series Books

N.W.A: The Aftermath

The Real Eminem: Broke City Trash Rapper

The Real Destiny's Child: The Writing's On The Wall

New York State of Mind 1.0

The Reasonings of Buju Banton, Bounty Killer & Sizzla

Magnolia: Home of tha Soldiers (Behind the Scenes with the Cash Money Millionaires)

The Real MC Eiht: Geah!

The Real Diddy

A Taste of The Real 213

Warren G and Nate Dogg created this G-Funk shit, and you hear it on - go listen to the radio. It's everywhere. Every time you hear me, you hear Warren G. That's who we are, that's where the sound came from. Everybody in the world is at my doorstep right now wanting a song. Everybody! Ask them when you interview 'em.

- Nate Dogg

Why now? Probably because we been waiting for so long actually to put out a 213 record, and now that we are able to do it, it's appropriate for right now. So, that's what the feeling is all about. Us expressing what we feel, that's what we feel.

- Snoop Dogg

I'm very happy. G-funk ain't went nowhere. It's still here.

- Warren G

Green for the money, gold for the honey. Being suited and booted from head to toe. Matching pieces. The shoes look like the suit; the suit looks like the shirt, the shirt looks like the hat. It's going down player. I'm the real deal. I got thirty years in this game. I ain't missed a day without checking paper from a female. They know I'm the real bling blinger. It ain't no joke.

- Bishop Don Magic Juan

Unearth the passion, grace, and mystery of Sean Combs, the apostle and avatar of pop culture, and one of the most complex Americans of the past half-century.

The Real Diddy, the 12th book in the series, captures an ambitious Sean Combs twice in the summer of 1999. It is the critical period in his life, fundamental to understand the thought process that precipitated his current success. The crossroads of life once entirely in sync with the music business and the shift to entertainment lifestyle capitalist.

Sean Combs empire and the influence that comes with leading a corner of pop culture is on a steady incline. Unfortunately, a bevvy of ugly personal rumours targets his essence as he faces second-degree assault and criminal mischief charges.

The Real Diddy unveils a core understanding of who Sean Combs is as a man, father, celebrity, artist, producer, entrepreneur and visionary. These critical reflections symbolise the turning point of Sean Combs life, IN HIS OWN WORDS!

There are hundreds of interviews and dozens of *Behind The Music Tales* series books to follow. That's why I am giving you a copy of *New York State of Mind 1.0* for FREE!

Join the Readers Group and get exclusive 1992 and 1993 interviews with Tragedy Khadafi, Brand Nubian, and Pete Rock & C.L. Smooth FREE!

I am only looking for your email. You will receive emails with updates on new releases, exclusive images, original audio, and be eligible for free advance copies of series books. You can opt out at any time.

http://eepurl.com/ckHZdb

www.ingramcontent.com/pod-product-compliance
Lightning Source LLC
Chambersburg PA
CBHW071541121125
35284CB00011B/453